Safe, Debt-Free, and Rich!

High-Return, Low-Risk Investing Strategies
That Can Make You Wealthy

Andrew Packer

Humanix Books

www.humanixbooks.com

Humanix Books

Safe, Debt-Free, and Rich: High-Return, Low-Risk Investing Strategies That Can Make You Wealthy
Copyright © 2018 by Humanix Books
All rights reserved

Humanix Books, P.O. Box 20989, West Palm Beach, FL 33416, USA
www.humanixbooks.com | info@humanixbooks.com

Library of Congress Control Number: 2017947286

Interior Design: Scribe Inc.

Humanix Books is a division of Humanix Publishing, LLC. Its trademark, consisting of the words "Humanix" is registered in the Patent and Trademark Office and in other countries.

Disclaimer: The information presented in this book is meant to be used for general resource purposes only; it is not intended as specific financial advice for any individual and should not substitute financial advice from a finance professional.

ISBN: 978-1-63006-078-7 (Paperback)
ISBN: 978-1-63006-079-4 (E-book)

Printed in the United States of America
10 9 8 7 6 5 4 3 2 1

To my mother, for her common sense, and to
my father, for his investment acumen

NO BOOK IS WRITTEN IN a vacuum. I'm grateful for the support of all my friends and family for tolerating me during the arduous writing process. Specifically:

At Newsmax: Christian Hill, Michael Berg, Stephanie Gallagher and Chris Ruddy.

At Humanix Books: Mary Glenn, Sherrie Slopianka, and the staff at Scribe.

Contents

Foreword

Why You Need This Guide

Bill Spetrino

I CONSIDER MYSELF AN INVESTOR first and foremost. I'm not an economist—I'm not some Wall Street broker trying to sell you on the latest hot stock. I'm just a normal guy who unlocked the secrets to investing and have put them to work for myself and, later on, for ordinary Americans looking to get better financial returns.

The most important thing you need to do with your money is manage it well. It's the difference between working for a living your entire life, or retiring comfortably . . . or even early, like I did at 42. That means finding the best opportunities and focusing on them to get the best returns. Few people get it.

Andrew Packer is one of the handful of people I've met who also gets it. He understands the importance of finding a great investment opportunity and how to best allocate capital to get the best returns. He always knows the right questions to ask before getting into any investment. He understands that there's more to the market than just numbers; there's a psychology to it too.

Most important, Andrew spends a lot of time thinking about what could go wrong before asking how much money he could make on a trade. Most people tend to see dollar signs in their future and plow in—only to end up underperforming the market or losing money.

Even though he's a young and generally quiet guy, he has an intuitive grasp of what you need to know when investing. In this latest book, *Safe, Debt-Free, and Rich: High-Return, Low-Risk Investing Strategies That Can Make You Wealthy*, Andrew will walk you through some of his best and most interesting trades. He'll explain why he selected those opportunities, what happened, and how he and his subscribers across various investment services made out as a result.

Throughout the book, you'll learn how to be a better investor. Best of all, you'll learn how to put that knowledge to use. By the time you're done, you'll have the knowledge you need to make better investment decisions, know when to exit a trade, and understand how to best maximize your returns while lowering your risk along the way.

Introduction

Investing Is about Reality, not Theory

WHILE THERE HAVE BEEN SOME great investors throughout history—and many of the best are still active today—to really understand how to be a great investor, we need to go back to the source of the most critical idea to hang on to during a wild investment lifetime.

Our story really begins with the Greek philosopher Plato. Plato asks us to imagine that we are bound and tied in a cave. Behind us is a fire or other source of light. Figures by the fire use objects to project images on the wall, not unlike a modern-day movie theater.

Plato tells us that this is our perception of reality. In this allegorical cave, we see the images of things, but not the substance. If we were to break free of our bonds, we would see how poorly they mimic the genuine article. We could then escape the cave and see the real world.

I'm often reminded of this allegory because investing is fundamentally about the truth. It's about determining what's really going on, not what you're being shown. In a world driven by 24/7 news coverage, irrelevant minutiae might be blown up until a better story comes along. And even then, what we're told about a story is usually framed through two lenses: fear and greed. A story about a robbery might be commonplace in a big city, but it can be played up relentlessly to create a culture of fear.

This shows that there's an emotional aspect to our lives as well. We need to not only see things as they truly are but be able to react to them appropriately and not merely in the way others expect us to.

When you can do that as an investor, there's an endless world of possibilities.

If you're looking to invest and not just trade, your investment journey starts with a world view. What does that mean? It's simply how you see the world and the factors shaping it. If your world view is accurate, or as close as possible, you'll be in a position to make realistic predictions about the future.

Since investing is about trying to gauge future trends today with some success, understanding where we are now is critical. After all, if you can't find where you are on a map, how will you get where you need to go?

Many traders might not even have a world view. To those who truly day-trade—and start and end the day in cash—every day, they have to rediscover what's going on. At the other end of the spectrum are those who invest by looking at longer-term trends that are in development. I'm firmly in the latter category. With so many traders chasing short-term gains (and often failing), looking toward the long term instead gives us a better edge and more time for an investment to successfully work out.

Right now, my world view looks at three major factors. Maybe I'm still in the cave, but I've found that if I look critically at these three factors when making investment decisions, I've gotten great results over time.

#1: What the Market Is Doing

This is a snapshot of the world. That's a pretty simple thing to find. Pull up a chart of the overall stock market—I like to use the

S&P 500 Index—and see what's going on. This is the basis of technical analysis, but you don't need to do anything too fancy.

In fact, you really only need to look at the direction that the market as a whole is moving to determine what about 80 percent of stocks are going to do at a given time. If the trend is going up, stocks will likely go up. If it's down, you'll want to wait for the line to stop going down if you're looking to buy again with less risk of a decline.

When the financial crisis ended in 2009, stocks had an immediate and powerful rally that eventually petered out. Over the past few years, the markets have been in a pattern where they've tended to trade sideways, fall around 10 percent or so, and then rally to break to new highs.

A sideways trend is no big deal—it means you can likely find individual bargains in the market and, for many positions, you can simply wait for a new trend to emerge and collect dividends in the meantime.

An extreme upward trend, one with a 45-degree angle or higher over six months, is usually a sign of a bubble forming. Stocks got extremely bullish and briefly exhibited this in 1929 and again in 2000. Many individual stocks can do this all the time, too, when they hit a faddish peak. The cryptocurrency Bitcoin made this move in early 2017, before tumbling back down. It's the only bullish trend that's likely a good reason for you to be bearish.

#2: What Nonmarket Participants Are Doing

I'd like to think that the market is really all that matters. But it isn't. A variety of nonmarket factors can influence the market as well. That includes political events, like elections in the United States and other Western nations. Surprise outcomes, like Britain voting to leave the European Union in June or Donald Trump's presidential win in 2016, can sometimes cause shock as folks make quick decisions about how to better invest in light of these new events.

The biggest factor by far is the Federal Reserve. Whole volumes have been written about it—and I've written extensively about its failure to stem off the financial crisis in my previous book, *Uncharted: Your Guide to Investing in the Age of Uncertainty*.

What matters right now is that the Fed has kept interest rates near zero since the financial crisis. They raised the prime interest rate (the rate most talked about and the one they charge to banks) from 0 percent to 0.25 percent in December 2015. When they did, markets had a six-week tantrum that led to a 10 percent decline in stocks before things turned around.

Why is such a small move such a big deal? Think about it this way: When bonds yield 5 percent, a bond with an annual payment (or coupon) of $5 trades at $100. When investors demand higher yields and move rates to 10 percent, that bond will need to trade at $50 for the $5 coupon to meet the new going rate of 10 percent.

In that example, the price had to fall by half. If you're a bond investor, right now, with interest rates so low and the Fed moving toward raising them, things look dangerous. But the alternative is to keep rates near zero, which also means ultralow interest rates on mortgages, car loans, and stock trades on margin. These low interest rates run the risk of overfueling the economy now, leading to a worse recession later.

Besides that danger, low interest rates mean bond yields are low, whether they're government, corporate, municipal, or junk bonds. Investors looking for yield aren't getting it from money market accounts or their checking or savings accounts either. Just think, 10 years ago, a savings account might yield 4 to 5 percent. Today, most yield less than 1 percent. That's a 75–80 percent loss of income from a safe place to secure your money!

That's pushed investors into stocks like utilities and telecoms. These highly regulated industries provide the most bond-like returns on the stock market. They're now becoming much more sensitive to interest rates as long as the current low-rate regime continues.

#3: What the Underlying Company Is Doing

Knowing what you're investing in matters. At the end of the day, a share of stock is one small fraction of an underlying business. Your best results as an investor will come from treating your investment decisions as though you were buying not just a share of stock but the entire company.

That's where fundamental analysis and valuation comes in. It's important to know what a company does, how they do it, and whether shares are cheap or expensive compared to their industry.

It means going through financial data like a company's revenues and cash flows, learning about their different divisions and how they interact. But it also includes noting important non-financial information like recent changes in the company's executive suite.

None of this information is static. Changes occur all the time. Most of the big changes occur four times a year, when companies report quarterly earnings.

Every sector also has its own quirks—those unusual trends that investors tend to watch to get an idea of how a company is doing relative to its competitors.

In the insurance industry, for instance, emphasis is placed on whether or not a company makes underwriting profits—the profits from writing policies before factoring in its portfolio of investments. If you're looking at a bank, you would want to look at its loan-loss reserves, a gauge of how much money it's setting aside in case it needs to write down loans with a dubious chance of being repaid. This information is part of a company's quarterly filings.

But even more unusual measures aren't. If you were looking to invest in a restaurant, you might want to look at seating turnover, or how many guests sit at the same table in a given night. That's the kind of criteria where physically going and investigating can provide an insight into an investment that a Wall Street analyst just can't get from the numbers.

Putting These Three Criteria Together

Armed with these three criteria, you should be able to get an idea of what's going on with the company you want to invest in, and whether or not that makes sense given its valuation, fundamentals, what others are doing, and what the market as a whole is doing.

It sounds simple, and to some extent it is. Aside from a little bit of knowledge and some math, what you really need is the conviction to stick to your world view amid an ever-changing environment. If you think that interest rates will eventually rise, you may be right. But that may take time, and it certainly won't happen in a straight line. There will be setbacks, and at many times, you'll likely question your decision.

In cases like that, before you think about selling out, at least stop and think about your world view criteria. If something's changed, you might be justified in closing the trade. If something's changed and it looks better or if nothing's changed but the overall valuation has improved, you might want to put more capital into the trade to increase your stake.

There are plenty of ways to think about a world view. And maybe you don't have a world view so much as a collection of ideas that add up to a world. There's nothing wrong with that. I tend to invest in what I believe the market's best opportunities are at a given time. The rationale might fit in with one part of a world view—like how the market is doing. Or it might be because of something ultraspecific to the company involved. It's creating an overall portfolio that fits your world view that matters, and different positions in your portfolio can do that in different ways.

When it comes down to it, recognizing what's really going on is what investing is all about. It allows you to recognize value when it exists and find new opportunities all the time without taking the risk of simply buying shares of a company and hoping for the best.

Let's jump ahead to see how these ideas all blend together. I'm going to take you on a quick journey—one that shows you what my average week looks like as I navigate the market and its various opportunities.

A Week in the Life

WHO AM I AND WHY do I matter? For the first part of that question, you'll find a short biography elsewhere in this book. But to really explain why I can help you find ways to safely and profitably invest in today's challenging environment, I want to walk you through one of my workweeks. To some extent, this week is typical of what I do week-in and week-out. But in reality, there is no typical or average week. Each is structured similarly but can vary wildly. Take a look.

Monday

It's 6:30 a.m., about sunrise. The stock market opens in three hours. I don't set an alarm. Rather, I'm woken up by the prodding of my two rescue cats. They're usually pretty sweet and affectionate, but for them, it's breakfast time.

After feeding them, I get up and get ready to head into Newsmax's headquarters, where I'm the senior financial writer. As I get in, I once again check the latest news. The European markets have been open for hours already and that will impact how markets in the United States open. I see that stocks look set to open generally flat.

I'm out of the house by 7:30, getting on the freeway typically while it's busy but hasn't slowed down substantially unless there's been an accident. Having grown up in the sprawl of Southern California, I feel like I've already put up with more than my fair share of traffic, and being ahead of the crowd means I can get a ton of work done before most people even show up for the day.

I get in the office before 8:00. It's early enough that it's still quiet, but I'm also not the first one in. Given my propensity for setting off alarms, that's fine with me. I look in more detail at some of the headlines that I saw at home.

I also look over an open portfolio of all the companies that I either personally own or have a trade out with one of my various investment services. I don't see anything in premarket trading that merits much of a closer look, but I make some notes to myself.

It looks like a busy week. Polls in the United Kingdom show the upcoming "Brexit" vote shifting in favor of leaving. The rise of national self-determination over a fully integrated global society seems to be a recurring theme in recent elections and polls—including the presidential contest in the United States.

I start jotting down some notes on what it could mean for any of my open positions either way. While I own a number of multinational firms, only a few have strong ties to Britain, with the biggest question mark being that of **Vodafone (VOD)**. As a telecom company, it should have reasonably consistent earnings no matter what the economy does or how this vote goes. They recently announced that they were buying telecom assets in New Zealand as well, so if anything, I'd be looking for any market panic on a Brexit as an opportunity to pick up more shares.

The market opens at 9:30 as always, and stocks are off and running. I see around 9:45 that a few options trades are faring well and that some stocks with a big sell-off this morning might make for a good options trade late in the day.

Throughout the day, it's a little bit of everything. I hear back from one of the other financial writers, who just put together an article for the monthly Financial Intelligence Report newsletter. Since I'm the only financial writer in-house at Newsmax, I'm often asked to fill in on anything where a background in financial markets, economics, and investing is required.

The article looks amazing. It's clear-cut and well written. It talks about the dangers investors face going into 2017. While I agree with a lot of the ideas and the article is well cited and sourced, it seems a bit pessimistic. I don't want one my colleagues to be wrong, per se, but I'm not sure conditions exist for another market crash—one that will unfold exactly like the 2008 global meltdown in stocks— that the writer is implying could happen here.

I get up around lunch to head to my car and read a few chapters of fiction. It's helpful to have breaks throughout the day, and if it weren't 84 degrees out, I'd be walking around the pond across the street from the office. It's easy to fall prey to laziness with a desk job, and that's not how I prefer to do things.

The afternoon is a bit quiet. On Mondays, everything that happens over the weekend tends to play out within the first hour of trading. The broad market is trending down following the last few weak trading days as well. I don't think a major correction is under way, but after a few weeks of the market steadily trading higher, it's time for a healthy pullback.

That's actually something that I've been predicting over the past few weeks. I note that two options trades I have for some of my two different investment services look ripe to take profits, as they've been rising while the overall market has turned south. Looking at the rest of the week, there's a Fed meeting on Wednesday, and Friday is an options expiration day. I make the call to close out the trades this week before those events potentially unwind the gains.

Early to work, early to leave. I head out at 5:00 p.m., again on the forefront of the evening traffic.

But that's not quite the end of my workday. Although I hit the sack around 11:30 p.m., I first eye the Asian markets, which have already opened for Tuesday. Financial markets are now open nearly all 24 hours of the day. What a time to be alive!

Tuesday

Once again I'm up near sunrise, checking out markets, and getting ready to head into the office. But on Tuesday mornings, it's time to put together the weekly update for my *Insider Hotline* newsletter investment service.

That means going through the notes I've been jotting down on Post-its all week regarding my thoughts on the broad market as well as our open positions. But this week's update is really about closing out a trade we made betting on higher volatility in the markets.

A month back, we bought a call option on the **iPath Volatility Index Short-Term Futures ETN (VXX)**. A week ago, that option was down nearly 50 percent, since market volatility remained low. But things have started to heat up in the past week, and the option is now up about 40 percent from where we bought it. While markets might trend down even more, there are a few events this week that could lead to a big rally. If that's the case, our gain could be a loss again.

Since I want to keep the profit we have and I'm not trying to get the absolute top of the trade, now's as good a time as any to close out the trade. By the time my trade alert is quickly edited and sent out by our speedy e-mail team, the market has opened and volatility is still on the rise. We'll end up making about a 50 percent return. That's not too shabby for an options trade that was down the week before, and that we've only held a month. Volatility trades are, well, volatile, and we can't expect to win on every trade.

Nevertheless, looking over the *Insider Hotline* portfolio's closed positions, this is the 17th winning trade in a row we've closed. To be fair, a number of positions in our open portfolio are currently down, but with time, I'm confident that all of them will end up as wins for us as well.

In the early afternoon, I field a few quick e-mails from our video team, who are putting the finishing touches on my most recent interview. I host a monthly interview show, *Profit Report*.

The week before, I spoke with commodities guru Jim Rogers for nearly an hour. Jim's a fantastic guy with a sharp wit, and even though he's more bearish about the economy than I am, he says it with a smile on his face because he has a plan to deal with it. I also like his humility—nearly every question I ask he'll respond to with a "Well, I'm not sure" or "You'd have to ask so-and-so." It's refreshing compared to some folks who act as though they know all the answers.

With a few details cleared up, the video will get posted online soon, available for subscribers of my financial services to enjoy.

After lunch, I stop by my publisher's office. We're working on a new service that launches soon, a monthly newsletter called *Crisis Point Investor*. The marketing material is coming along nicely and I want to check in on a few things to make sure we're on the same page. It's important that my thoughts on the upcoming issue I'm working on fit well with what we're putting together. Also on Tuesday afternoons, the Newsmax financial team meets for a quick phone call so that everyone can check in. It's a pretty quiet week, with no major issues.

Markets close; the workday takes a reprieve for the evening. The Asian markets look quiet as I head to bed.

Wednesday

Like Tuesday mornings, the early part of Wednesday focuses on another weekly update, this one for the *Financial Braintrust*. In this investment service, my main focus is on best-of-breed companies in their industry. That sometimes means paying more than I'd like as a value investor, but over time, investing in the best has led to superior returns.

This week we're closing out an options trade as well. This is a two-month-old trade betting on higher prices for the gold miners. While there are a few standout gold mining companies, we bet on the sector as a whole because it's a very small sector and because gold has been in an uptrend since the start of 2016. This trade—the **VanEck Vectors Gold Miners ETF (GDX)**—was up more than 70 percent from where we bought it when it closed yesterday. It's also been a steadier trade than the *Insider Hotline* trade on volatility.

But with gold closing in on $1,300 and with a Federal Reserve meeting this afternoon, gold could take a dive. Sure, it could go higher as well, but why let a profit disappear? I put out an order to close out the options trade here as well.

By the end of the day, the Fed's comments and refusal to raise interest rates have led to a surge in gold, and our total return on this options trade ends up at a staggering 109 percent. That's a fantastic return, especially since we bought far out-of-the-money call options and we've had to offset declining time premium for two months. Owning an option like this is like holding a hot potato—if you have it for too long, you can end up getting burned.

Besides the trade alert, I look out over the next few months. We have a few stock positions in our portfolio where we've sold covered call options. That's a way of earning extra income on companies we already own at the possible price of being called away from our shares. These positions, in the utility and insurance space, have been popular since the start of the year, and overall valuations are getting high. So I don't mind that happening.

In the afternoon, the aforementioned Fed meeting and press conference with Chairwoman Janet Yellen holds my attention. It's now June, and the Fed hasn't raised interest rates since December. That means they probably won't raise rates any higher ahead of the election.

In turn, that means that traders will likely gravitate toward stocks since they represent the best game in town on a risk-adjusted basis. In other words, it's better to put your money in a utility stock paying a 3 percent dividend for 10 years compared to owning a 10-year treasury that yields 1.66 percent. The income is nearly twice as good, and over a 10-year period, you're not likely to lose money on a capital gains basis (of course, over a shorter period, anything is possible).

The Fed results are a little disappointing, as many Fed officials have been hinting since the last meeting that rates might go up in June. It makes me wonder—yet again—about the central bank's credibility. I jot down a few quick thoughts on the matter.

Thursday

I don't have a weekly update or trade alert on Thursdays, but it is my day for writing a blog that posts Friday. This week, it's all about yesterday's Fed meeting and what it means for investors looking ahead to the rest of the year.

I add in some thoughts on volatility, which is still on my mind following this week's closed trade for *Insider Hotline*, as well as the fact that it's still on the rise following the lackluster meeting—they need a better PR person to address the press at the Fed. While the chairwoman and governors are intelligent people, they'd have better public support if they were able to speak more clearly and plainly. I always try to keep my thoughts at or under a 10th-grade reading level to keep it accessible—the Fed should do the same.

Then again, former Fed Chairman Alan Greenspan once said, "If you think you understood what I just said, you misheard me." So perhaps being misleading is one of the Fed's goals. If that's the case, it's a disservice to investors.

In any event, the blog goes through a few different versions before I find a combination of ideas I'm happy with.

Thursdays are also a catch-up day to look beyond developing news and stock prices and get into some heavier research. On docket for the day are some articles I've bookmarked but haven't gotten to yet. The topics range from companies with "moats" (a competitive advantage that others can't compete with) to what some value investors and fund managers are doing now to some thoughts on the upcoming vote on whether or not Britain should leave the European Union.

It's been my experience that you can't be a good writer without being a good reader, and getting through this backlog of articles takes time. That's no big deal, though. While the topics are all over the place, my view is that everything's interconnected. It's the strength of the connection, and the relative importance of other events at the time, that will impact your investment returns.

While I'm getting through my reading, I also hear back from one of my editors on the latest issue of *Crisis Point Investor*. We go back and forth a bit on the lead—a fantastic but true story about how one company, Teledyne, bought back more than 80 percent of its outstanding shares. As a result, shareholders made thousands of percent returns in profits during a time when the broad market churned sideways.

I think today's corporate buyback programs aren't as effective, and my editor agrees with that premise, so she thinks a different lead would be better. We stick with the Teledyne lead—investors need to know what to look for in a great buyback program and what to avoid. Most of the meat and potatoes of the issue is what to avoid, so I think it provides a good counterbalance. With that and a few minor changes, the issue is now on its way to our graphics team to be laid out and designed.

After the market close, a company we own in our *Crisis Point Investor* portfolio reports earnings. The company is **Smith & Wesson Holding Corporation (SWHC)**, a firearms manufacturer. Firearms sales have been on the rise, according to the latest FBI background check statistics, and shares have bene up and down sharply all week following an act of radical Islamic terrorism over the prior weekend in Orlando.

But the company's operating numbers are what matters over time, and they're solid. Shares go up about 10 percent in after-hours trading, adding to the slight gain shares have already had in an otherwise challenging week for the markets.

Friday

I start my day with something of a personal task—managing my trading account. It's the third Friday of June and therefore options expiration day. I don't have any put options expiring, but I have a number of covered calls in the energy space that look like they're about to expire at zero.

Since the start of the year, I've been experimenting with a new strategy. I often like to try out new ideas and strategies with real money as quickly as possible to see how they work in the real world, and this is the account I use. The new strategy I've been playing with recently is to add to losing stock positions I've had in the energy space. In February, oil hit a short-term bottom and it's been trending higher ever since. Many energy stocks are up 60, 80, or even double off their lows.

I'm skeptical that the trend can continue, but by buying more shares earlier in the year, I've lowered my cost basis. Now I have a conundrum: take short-term profits, or shoot for a steady-ish income? I've gone for the income, selling covered call options against half the open position.

If I'm called away, I'll be taking a big gain compared to where I bought shares earlier in the year. But compared to a few years ago, it'll still be a loss. And with the short-term income from the call options, I'm looking at getting an extra 10–15 percent returns in the space of a few months by selling at-the-money call options.

For instance, I bought some shares of the Brazilian oil giant **Petrobras (PBR)** back in 2014 when it was in the teens. It closed to near $20 ahead of the elections there, but took a big dive when the incumbent anticapitalist government won. It certainly didn't help that oil prices started taking a big dive thereafter.

But at the start of the year, shares were down to $3, far below where the company was worth operationally, and even below where it'd be worth in bankruptcy. So I bought shares around $4. In the past few months, they've been in the $5–7 range.

But I'm not too greedy; I've been selling covered call options with a strike price of $6. That's a 50 percent gain if I'm called away from the $4 shares—and within the space of a few months. Add in the $1 in premium I sold, and that's another 15 percent gain. I've already done this once this year, and I figure a 15 percent return of my capital in cash every 6–8 weeks is well worth it. Shares have been between $5.50 and $6.50 lately, but they're under $6, so today's options will expire at zero—and I'll sell a new set of call options Monday, possibly at the $7 strike price if oil prices rally next week.

I do something similar with another down position, **Transocean (RIG)**, which I've had for about a year. Shares are around $10, and my cost basis is $15, but I've made about $4 per share income from covered call writing since I bought, so things don't look as bad there.

With this checkup to my trading portfolio done, I'm on to another round of research.

In the early afternoon, a powerful thunderstorm blows by the office. A car in the parking lot gets hit by lightning—not mine. Given the inclement weather, I opt to work through lunch.

A family member e-mails in the afternoon. He likes **Apple (AAPL)** and wonders what I think about put options. I already trade options for my family in an account of theirs and point out that we have four trades in total, two of which are put options expiring *next* month. I suggest holding for now. There's still about $1.50 in option premium in the July puts, so between that and the costs of closing out the existing trade and opening a new one, we're better off doing nothing. Sometimes, if not most of the time, that's the best bet with your investments.

The market closes flat for the day but still down for the week. There've been a number of short-term fears—that never changes. It's the specific short-term fears that matter, as well as their potential importance on an investment portfolio. That'll always vary.

That wraps up another workweek. It's typical for me . . . but never the same. Just like the world of investing in general. I wouldn't have it any other way.

In a nutshell, that's who I am. I'm plugged into the markets day after day, watching millions of people make millions of decisions in real-time, and trying to figure out my own path. My path as an investor is determined by several factors. The biggest factor that I have to contend with is the same that others have to contend with as well—the role that central banking plays in our lives. Far from just helping or hurting the stock market, it influences prices in everything we buy or sell.

Recap

Investing 101

Before we get into the nuts and bolts of successful trades and what to look for, novice investors, or even seasoned pros, may want a quick refresher on some basic investment concepts and terms. If you're already familiar with the language of Wall Street and are ready to learn about how to make safe, debt-free, and wealth-creating investments, then feel free to skip to the next section.

1. What Is Investing, and What Are the Risks?

AN INVESTMENT IS ANYTHING THAT you buy based on a reasonable belief, or expectation, that it will leave you financially better off in the future.

Every investment entails risk. Every investment takes time. You must be prepared for both.

Financial risk usually means you may lose some or all of your investment. But even so-called risk-free assets, such as Treasury bonds, are not truly as riskless as many believe. They face inflation risk. When investors say Treasurys are risk-free, they really mean free from *default* risk, which means you're guaranteed to get your money back plus interest. The government can deliver that promise since it has the ability to print money. Promising that those dollars will have more purchasing power, however, is a different story. It's one of the biggest risks in all financial plans and, unfortunately, one of the most overlooked.

Time is the second factor common to all investments. True financial investing requires time, usually months or years, before you have any chance of realizing your expected gains. That's because a true investment is an investment in economic growth.

Any investment designed to make money quickly is not a true investment but, instead, speculation or gambling.

2. Are Stocks a Good Investment?

A study by finance and economics professor Jack Clark Francis at Baruch College in New York, found that for the 30-year period covering 1978 to 2008, the S&P 500 Index (my preferred way to measure the overall stock market) returned an average of 13.4 percent. Housing came in at 8.6 percent. Nothing else was close—not commercial real estate, bonds, futures, or mortgage securities.

Despite the recent market turbulence, you just can't find a better place to get the returns offered by stocks.

To meet financial goals, most investors use stocks, bonds, and mutual funds. But there are other asset classes such as commodities (gold, oil, silver, wheat, etc.). There is also the foreign currency market, also called forex. Then there are derivatives, such as options (like the covered call options I like to write) and futures. A derivative is any asset whose value is tied to, or derived from, the value of another asset or index. For this guide, we will concentrate on stock investing.

3. What Are Shares of a Company?

What exactly are shares of stock? How does one become a shareholder?

Corporations can transfer ownership easily, which allows them to raise cash quickly. Corporations do this by dividing the company into pieces; each piece is called a *share*. Anyone who owns a share owns part of the company.

To raise cash quickly, corporations can "go public," which, in the United States, means registering with the SEC (Securities and Exchange Commission) along with jumping through a few other regulatory hoops.

Corporations must also meet certain listing requirements. For example, to be listed on the Nasdaq, it must have at least 400 shareholders, one million shares available, and revenues of $10 million or more over the past three years. Each stock exchange has its own requirements, but they are fairly rigid, partly to ensure that people aren't just listing corporations that are nothing but a piece of paper.

Offering shares of a corporation for sale to the public creates a *publicly traded company*, which means it's no longer a private business. Anyone who wants to be a part owner can become one by simply buying shares.

4. What Does the Term *Stock Market* Actually Refer To?

The stock market is the marketplace—the secondary market—where shares are traded.

The big business brand names you're familiar with are all likely to be publicly traded—Wal-Mart, Coca-Cola, Exxon Mobil, Microsoft, and Apple.

Whenever you buy shares of stock, you are buying shares that were once owned by another investor. You're not buying the shares directly from the company; that's only during the initial public offering (IPO) or secondary offerings.

Having the ability to buy into big-name businesses is one of the biggest advantages of stock market investing. Rather than taking your money and investing it in a start-up company (that has a high chance of failing), you can invest that money in a successful company. There's no work, no schedules, no employees. You just own part of the company and reap the rewards of the company's success. Can you make money this way?

If you had purchased 100 shares of Microsoft for $21 during its IPO in 1986, after all the stock splits and price adjustments, in August 2015, you'd have 28,800 shares valued at close to $44 each, for a total value just over $1.2 million. And that's not counting dividends.

Unfortunately, most investors think the stock market is a way to get rich quickly. Yes, it can happen. But if you're looking for quick money, it's speculation.

True investments in great companies, though, can work magic over time. The key words? *Over time*. We'll look at some specific examples of that in more detail.

5. What Are the NYSE and Nasdaq?

When a business becomes publicly traded, it's traded on an exchange such as the *New York Stock Exchange* (NYSE) or the *Nasdaq*. While their business models may be quite different, all exchanges ultimately try to do the same thing: they aim to be centralized meeting places where investors can publicly post orders to buy and sell shares.

Originally, exchanges were done in person and on paper. With the advent of computers, a second type of exchange emerged: the electronic exchange. There is no physical address but, instead, just a bunch of computers linked together where market makers and investors may post quotes to buy and sell. The most popular is the Nasdaq.

There is another category of exchange you should understand, which is the OTCBB, or *Over the Counter Bulletin Board*. While it's owned by Nasdaq, the over-the-counter market is entirely different from other exchanges. It's the Wild West of the stock market, where shares of stock trade that don't meet the listing requirements of the physical exchanges or Nasdaq. They may even be stocks in bankruptcy.

6. What Are Ticker Symbols?

Before you can buy or sell shares of a publicly traded company, you'll need the stock's *ticker symbol*, which is a unique identifying symbol.

Your broker's platform will have search features that allow you to type the company name and find the ticker. You can easily find tickers by searching the Internet too.

Ticker symbols are usually made up of one to four letters. For example, AT&T trades under T, General Motors uses GM, and IBM uses IBM, and eBay uses—you guessed it—EBAY.

Some tickers contain a fifth letter to designate other information. For instance, if the fifth letter is *Q*, it shows the company is in bankruptcy. The letter *Y* is used to denote an American Depositary Receipt (ADR), which is a foreign stock that trades on a US exchange. For example, Nestlé is based in Switzerland, but you can buy ADR shares in the United States under the ticker NSRGY.

7. How Do You Make Money from Stocks?

You have two ways to make money from stocks: capital appreciation and dividends.

Capital appreciation (or capital gains) results from buying low and selling high. The difference between your selling price and purchase price acts as interest on your investment. To judge performance, you'll want to calculate the *return on investment* (ROI) for each investment, as well as the overall portfolio. How do you calculate the ROI?

The amount you invest is called the principal. If you buy stock for $50 per share and sell it for $60 per share, your return is $10 per share, or 20 percent ($10/$50).

Returns, however, are always expressed as if the investment was held for one year, which is called *annualizing*. If you made 20 percent on your investment in six months, then your investment performed much better than 20 percent per year. To annualize this return, just figure out how many six-month periods are in one year, which is two. Therefore, your return is twice as good, or 2 * 20 percent = 40 percent annualized.

If you held the investment for only three months, your annualized return would be 4 * 20 percent = 80 percent since there are four three-month periods in one year. Annualizing works in reverse if you held the investment more than one year. If you earned 20 percent over a two-year period, your annualized return is 10 percent per year.

The second way to make money from stock is through *dividends*. Companies often return a portion of earnings to investors (owners) by paying a dividend. A dividend is just an ongoing periodic cash payment to investors. But not all companies pay dividends. Many companies, especially start-ups, like to retain all earnings and plow them back into the business.

8. How Can I Evaluate a Stock?

What makes a stock a "good deal?" People have different opinions and styles that can be broken down into two camps. First, there is *fundamental analysis*, which attempts to break down a company via its financial statements. This aims to figure out the health and value of a business as compared to its stock price. The second kind is *technical analysis*, which uses a multitude of formulas and figures to analyze trends on a stock's price chart to determine the most likely next move.

9. How Do I Choose a Brokerage Firm?

While there are many brokers choose from, they fall into two basic categories: full-service brokers and discount brokers. Full-service firms include the big names you're probably familiar with, like Goldman Sachs, Merrill Lynch, Morgan Stanley Smith Barney, and Prudential Securities.

Full-service brokers primarily make their money by offering investment banking services, which includes raising money by taking private companies public (IPO), making secondary offerings, assisting with mergers and acquisitions, and bond sales. But investors can open accounts to buy and sell shares of stock and other financial assets.

Stock commissions can run $100, $200, or more just to buy 100 shares. And you'll pay it again to sell. Because of the intense competition from discount brokers, some full-service brokers advertise special trading accounts where you can trade an unlimited amount of shares for no commissions. But there's always a catch. They charge a fixed percentage of assets, which usually runs 1 percent to 1.5 percent per year. If you have a $1 million account, it's going to cost between $10,000 and $15,000 per year to trade "commission free."

Full-service firms also have hefty asset requirements just to open an account, and may not accept an application if you plan to bring less than $1 million in assets—maybe more.

Full-service brokers get their fiercest competition from the *discount brokers*. Sometimes they're called *online brokers* since they usually require investors to place orders over the Internet, or through proprietary software. By reducing the need for brokers, discounters offer low commissions, some below $5 a trade—no matter how many shares you buy.

However, if you're not comfortable placing your own trades, most offer broker-assisted trades but charge a higher commission. Rather than paying $5 per trade, it may be closer to $40.

Discounter brokers include TD Ameritrade, E*Trade, Scottrade, Charles Schwab, and Fidelity. Like their full-service counterparts, discounters have required minimums to open an account, but because of competitive pressures, their minimums are low. Many will open an account with as little as $500.

In comparison, our newsletters, like *Insider Hotline* or the *Braintrust*, will provide all the information you need to place orders—and with no biases. We don't promote stocks. We don't hold stocks in inventory. If one of our editors owns or is looking to buy a specific stock they're writing about, they'll disclose that. And we definitely don't have institutional clients that we must cater to. We have one focus—you. The only way we make money is by making you money.

10. How Do I Open an Account?

Regardless of whether you choose a full-service or online broker, opening an account is easy. Most allow online applications, but some may require you to mail an actual signature rather than a digital signature over the Internet. It's an easy form to fill out—usually about five or six pages. If your broker has a local office, you can open an account in minutes and begin investing that day. Most just require a check, and will let you invest it before it has even cleared. You will be asked to provide personal information such as annual income and liquid net worth. The Financial Industry Regulatory Authority (FINRA) is the self-regulatory agency overseeing brokerage firm and broker conduct. FINRA Rule 2090 is the *Know Your Customer Rule* and FINRA Rule 2111 is a new *Suitability Rule*. These rules require brokers to know customers' financial positions before allowing them to invest. If you have a dispute with your broker, you're required to arbitrate through FINRA, and falsifying required information won't gain you sympathy. Be sure to fill out the form accurately.

11. What Is Margin on an Account?

The account application will also ask if you want to add *margin* to your account. It's usually just a simple box to check yes or no. A margin account allows you to use stocks, bonds, mutual funds, or other assets as collateral for borrowing money, which can be used for anything you'd like, from buying a new car to buying more shares.

Regulation T, or Reg. T for short, is the law governing the extension of credit in margin accounts. Currently, it requires investors to pay for at least 50 percent of the trade, subject to a $2,000 minimum. For example, if you buy $10,000 worth of stock in a margin account, you're only required to deposit $5,000 and would pay interest on the remaining $5,000. You can certainly pay for any trade in full and won't be charged interest; margin accounts just give you the option to borrow.

Investors usually have margin accounts to provide financial leverage, which just means gains are magnified—but so are losses. For example, assume you buy 100 shares of stock outright for $100 for a total of $10,000. If the price rises 10 percent to $110, you earned $1,000, or 10 percent. However, if you only deposited $5,000 to pay for the trade, you'd earn the same $1,000 gain while putting up only a $5,000 investment. So your leveraged return would be 20 percent—exactly double. It's double because you only paid for half the trade but controlled 100 percent of the shares.

If the investment falls $1,000, you'd lose 20 percent instead of 10 percent. The biggest risk for investors is to borrow heavily against margin accounts and have the account equity hovering near the house percent. One swift downturn in the market and your broker will be calling to deposit more money—possibly a lot.

12. What Are the Forms of Ownership I Need to Choose From?

Besides selecting the type of account, you will be asked on the account application to designate a *form of ownership*. You can choose between *Joint Tenants with Rights of Survivorship* (JTWROS) or *Tenants in Common* (TIC). For JTWROS, if one account holder dies, the assets become the immediate possession of the surviving account holder or holders. The assets just roll over equally to the remaining names. The advantage is that it's a great way to avoid probate.

If you select tenants in common, assets are held either equally or unequally. Two people, for example, may share the assets 50–50, but they could also choose other distributions. If one account holder dies, the designated percentage of assets reverts to his or her estate. This allows assets to remain within the family.

13. How Do I Fund an Account?

Once you've opened your account, you'll need to fund it before you place trades. Firms will accept personal checks, and most do not require it to clear before placing trades. Just deposit the check and place your orders. However, brokers will also accept cashier's checks, stock, or bond deposits (if you're holding the certificates in a safe deposit box, for example), or transfers from other brokers or banks.

If you already have a broker and want to switch to another, transferring assets is easy. Just fill out an ACAT (Automated Customer Account Transfer) form at the receiving broker and they'll handle the rest. It usually takes about two to three weeks for transfers to complete. Just be careful if you have any proprietary funds or assets, as not all brokers will hold them. For instance, if you have the Merrill Lynch Emerging Markets Fund, it probably won't transfer to E*Trade.

Before using an ACAT, it's a good idea to sit with the receiving broker and see which assets they will hold.

Another method used to transfer securities is the Depository Trust & Clearing Corporation (DTCC), sometimes called a DTC transfer. The DTCC is the National Securities Clearing

Corporation (NSCC), which is designed to clear and settle transactions. While you usually won't be able to use this service to transfer an entire account, it can be used to transfer assets from one broker to another. Just keep that in mind should you need a simple transfer, for example, 100 shares of stock between brokers. DTC transfers are usually completed in a matter of hours.

But if you have an existing account with shares of stock, bonds, ETFs (exchange traded funds), most mutual funds—certainly cash—or just about anything that can be traded in the open market, you will most likely be able to transfer it to another broker.

14. What Is a Stock Quote?

The financial markets are continuous, live auctions where investors compete to buy and sell shares. Prices flicker constantly—up a bit, down a bit. Whenever you are entering an order, you will always see two prices, the *bid price* and *asking price* (also called an *offer price*), as shown below:

BID	ASK
$20	$20.30

The bid and ask represent the *quote.* Let's say the above bid and ask is for ABC stock. If you ask your broker for a quote on ABC, he'll say it's bidding $20 and asking $20.30.

The bid shows the *highest* price that another investor somewhere in the world is willing to pay at that moment. For any auction, whether Sotheby's, eBay, or the stock market, buyers place bids.

The asking price shows the *lowest* price at which another investor somewhere in the world is willing to sell at that moment. If you're selling a home, you'd say you were asking such-and-such a price. Sellers place asking prices.

Looking at the above quote, an investor somewhere is willing to sell shares for $20.30 per share. If you're willing to pay that price, the order can be executed. That's the price you can pay—at least right now. It could change, up or down, in the next second.

Likewise, the above quote shows that some investor is willing to buy shares for $20 per share. If you're willing to receive that price, the order can be executed. That's the price you can currently receive, but it too can change quickly.

The difference between the bid and ask is called the *bid-ask spread*. In this example, it's $0.30. The narrower the spread, the more competitive the auction. Most of the larger, well-known stocks may trade with 1-cent spreads or slightly wider.

Where do the bid and asking prices come from? They come from investors around the world—people just like you—entering what are called "limit orders." Whenever you enter an order, you must specify the price you're willing to pay, if buying, or receive if selling. You have two choices: market order or limit order. Let's begin with placing an order first before getting into the details.

15. How Do I Place an Order?

All brokers have websites or software that allow you to enter trades. Most offer broker-assisted trades, which means you can place the trade by calling a broker. It's called "assisted" since the broker will not give specific advice on what to buy or when to sell. Instead, they listen to your needs and help you select the type of order that is best for you.

For that extra help, you'll probably pay a higher commission, perhaps $40 rather than $5 for using the web. If you're brand new to investing, it's not a bad idea to use a broker for the first few trades for added security. But you'll find it's incredibly easy once you understand the lingo.

16. What Does It Mean When I Enter a Market Order to Buy a Stock?

A *market order* guarantees that you will buy or sell the shares, but it doesn't guarantee the price. Remember, prices fluctuate. A market order just instructs the broker to execute, or fill, the order—and let price fall where it may.

If you're buying shares, you should reference the asking price. In the above quote, you can currently buy shares for $20.30. However, if you place a market order, you're not guaranteed to pay that price—it might move—whether up or down at the very second you send the order.

By using a market order though, you know one thing for sure: you're definitely getting the order filled. The trade-off is that you have to be flexible on price. To buy 100 shares of ABC, you would give the following instructions: **"Buy 100 shares of ABC at market."** The second the order is sent, you'll get a confirmation in a matter of seconds showing the price you actually paid.

17. How Do I Sell Shares of Stock That I Own?

How would you sell ABC shares? In our example, the current bid is $20. If you had shares to sell and placed a market order, you would definitely sell your shares, but it's possible you won't receive exactly $20—the price might move up or down. The instructions to give your broker would be **"Sell 100 shares of ABC at market."** When the order is sent, you'll know the exact price received in seconds. Anytime you must get the order filled, you have no choice but to use a market order.

In contrast to market orders, *limit orders* allow you to specify an exact price—a limit—at which you're willing to pay if buying or receive if selling. Limit orders guarantee that you won't pay more than your limit if buying or receive less than your limit if selling.

They don't, however, guarantee your order will be filled. You may put in a limit order at $20.05 and never see it filled.

If you wish to buy 100 shares of ABC and want to be assured you will not be spending more than the $20.30 asking price, you would give the broker the following order: **"Buy 100 shares of ABC at a limit of $20.30."** This order can only be filled for $20.30 or less. The risk is that if the price moves when you send the order, it may never fill.

On the other hand, if you want to sell shares of ABC and don't want to receive less than the $20 bid, you would tell the broker, **"Sell 100 shares of ABC at a limit of $20."** This order can only be filled if the broker can get $20 per share—or more. The risk is that the order may not fill.

18. What Is a Stop Order and a Stop-Limit Order?

Sometimes, our newsletter writers will recommend hedging risk by using two special types of orders called a *stop order* and a *stop-limit order*. Such orders allow for automatic sales if a stock hits a certain price, usually when it's falling. After all, not every trade works out. When prices fall, we may decide to cut our losses and move on to a better opportunity. But what if the price is falling and you aren't in front of the computer to enter the order? Or maybe you're in a business meeting and can't call the broker.

This is where stop and stop-limit orders come in. A stop order is a *separate order* to sell your shares but only if a certain stock price is reached. For a stop order, you enter a price below the current stock price, which is called the *stop price*. If the stock's price ever trades at that price—or below—it triggers the order and the computer submits a *market order*. That's important to understand: stop orders convert to market orders.

Say you purchased 100 shares of ABC for $20 per share and want to sell them if the stock trades at or below $18. Here's what you'd tell the broker: **"Sell 100 shares of ABC at a stop of $18."**

The important point to understand about the stop price is that if the stock's price touches or crosses that line, the computer submits a market order. Because it's a market order, you cannot be assured of receiving $18 per share.

In the above example, traders often believe that if they purchased shares for $20 and placed a stop at $18, they are guaranteed to limit their loss to the $2 difference. That's far from true. The stock may close at $18.10 today and not trigger the order. But bad news may be announced before the opening bell tomorrow, and the stock opens for trading at $15. Because $15 is at or below the $18 stop, it will trigger the order, and your order is going to be filled at that market price.

Is there a way to guarantee price? Sure, but you cannot guarantee the execution. To guarantee the price, you can place a *stop-limit* order, which you do by telling the broker *two* prices: a stop price and a stop-limit price: **"Sell 100 shares of ABC at a stop of $18, with a stop limit of $17.50."**

The stop price serves the same function as it does for the stop order. It's nothing but a trigger point. With the above order, if the stock trades at the stop price of $18 or lower, the order is triggered. But rather than submitting a market order, the computer sends a limit order to sell at the $17.50 stop-limit price. The order can only be filled for $17.50 or more. It's just a standard limit order once submitted; it's not guaranteed to fill.

Which should you use, a stop or stop limit? If you feel you definitely want out of the trade—regardless of the price you'd receive—use a stop order. It's the only way to be assured that you will exit the trade if your stop price is triggered. But if there's a price at which you'd rather hold the shares, use a stop limit.

19. Can You Explain the Time Limit Options I Have When Placing an Order to Purchase Stock?

Whenever you place any type of order, you must always designate a time limit that the trade is allowed to stand. You have two choices: *day* and *good-til-canceled* (GTC). A day order is good only for the trading day, which ends at 4:00 p.m. ET. If the order is not filled at that time, it's automatically canceled. If you want to try again the next day, you'd have to reenter the order.

If you choose GTC, the order will continue to reinstate itself each trading day until filled or until you cancel it. While GTC orders can technically remain open indefinitely, some brokers have restricted time limits, perhaps 30 or 60 days. If the order is not filled within the broker's allotted time, it's then canceled.

20. How Should I Decide How Many Shares to Buy?

Investors have several decisions to make with every order, but the most important one is the trade size, or *investment allocation*. New investors often think the decision is easy: buy 100 shares; if you can afford more, buy in multiples of 100. It's one of the most dangerous beliefs in all of investing.

Because stocks trade at different prices, always buying 100 shares means that investors allocate different dollar amount to different investments. If ABC is trading for $20 per share and XYZ is trading for $100 per share, then 100-share purchases result in a $2,000 and a $10,000 investment respectively. Here's the problem . . .

If ABC rises 50 percent and XYZ falls 20 percent, it's tempting to think your portfolio is doing well since the percentage gains are bigger than the losses. But you've lost money. A 50 percent increase in ABC results in a $1,000 gain, but a 20 percent drop in XYZ leaves you with a $2,000 loss. Your $12,000 investment in the two stocks is now worth $11,000. What can you do to improve performance?

Instead of focusing on a fixed number of shares, focus on the dollars invested. If you split your $12,000 into two trades of $6,000 what would have happened? With ABC at $20, you could buy 300 shares. For XYZ trading at $100, you could only buy 60 shares. Both positions, however, have identical dollars invested, and that will change the outcome.

With ABC up 50 percent, you've earned $3,000. And with XYZ down 20 percent, you've lost $1,200. Overall, your portfolio is up $1,800 and has increased from $12,000 to $13,800. That's a big difference compared to falling to $11,000.

Definitions of Investment Types

Common Stock: Owning common shares, or a piece of the company, provides many benefits. First, you have the potential for unlimited gains. Second, as a common stock holder, your risk is limited to the dollars invested, unlike corporate insiders, who can be subject to liabilities. Although it's unlikely for the stock's price to become zero, it is the maximum risk. Another benefit is that many stocks pay dividends.

Bonds: Bonds are nothing more than an IOU issued by a corporation. Companies issue bonds to borrow from the investing public. They get your money today from the sale, promising to pay back the loan plus a certain interest rate, which is usually fixed. However, some bonds use *floating* interest rates where they will pay more if interest rates increase and less if they fall. Bonds are generally sold in $1,000-face increments, which is called *par value*. They are also sold with different due dates, which is called the *maturity*, which can range anywhere between one month and 50 years.

Preferred Stock: Preferred stock is like a hybrid between common stock and bonds. Preferred shareholders give up their right to corporate earnings, with the exception of dividends. Just as bonds are issued at $1,000 par value, preferred shares are usually issued at $25 per share. The dividend amount determines the yield. If the company pays $2.50 per year, it would be listed as a $2.50 dividend / $25 face value = 10 percent preferred stock. The $2.50 dividend would normally be divided into four payments over the year, although some companies pay monthly.

Mutual Fund: A professionally managed basket of stocks. Mutual funds have low minimum requirements. You may be able to buy into a fund with as little as $1,000 and make subsequent purchases with as little as $100. Mutual funds are great ways to build portfolios over time. Another benefit is diversification. Because the fund owns many different companies, if one company goes bankrupt, or faces a sharp drop in its price, it won't affect the fund's value that much.

Exchange Traded Fund (ETFs): An ETF is essentially a mutual fund that trades like a stock. Its price will fluctuate constantly through the day, and you can buy and sell at any time. The main thing to understand about ETFs is that they are a great way to buy a single "stock" but actually own many stocks since you're technically buying a fund. You get immediate diversification but only have to manage one security. Another benefit is that most ETFs have lower expense ratios than their mutual fund counterparts.

Real Estate Investment Trusts (REIT): Real estate is expensive and few people can afford a diversified basket of properties. Even if you could afford such a portfolio, it would be difficult to manage so many properties across the United States—or the world. The financial markets offer a great solution, which is called the real estate investment trust, or REIT (pronounced "reet"). Through REITs, investors can purchase real estate equity, which is the same idea for stocks but just applied to real estate. REITs are similar to ETFs since they trade like a stock on an exchange.

Master Limited Partnership (MLP): Essentially a limited partnership that trades like a stock. To encourage investment in energy exploration, Congress created the MLP structure by passing the Tax Reform Act of 1986 and the Revenue Act of 1987. The most significant hurdle for an MLP is that it must obtain at least 90 percent of its income from "qualified sources," which include real estate, natural resources, or minerals.

Common Analysis Terms Defined

Price-to-Earnings Ratio (P/E): The stock's current price divided by the earnings per share (EPS). If a stock is currently $40 and EPS is $2, then the P/E is 20. This ratio shows how much investors are willing to pay for $1 worth of earnings. If a company has losses for the quarter (negative earnings), you may see the P/E reported as negative or N/A for "not applicable."

Book Value: The cash value of the company or the value "carried on the books" and sometimes called the carry value. To calculate the book value, the company takes the total value contributed by investors and depreciates its assets. The book value shows the value that shareholders would receive if the company was liquidated.

Price-to-Book Value: The company's share price divided by the book value. It shows what investors are willing to pay for $1 worth of tangible assets.

Return on Equity (ROE): The year's earnings divided by the average shareholder equity. All things equal, it's better to have a higher ROE, as it shows the relative value that management created with investors' equity. Still, a company that uses a lot of debt (by selling bonds) will have a higher ROE, but that is due to the debt leverage rather than management performance.

Free Cash Flow (FCF): The cash that a company produces from its operations minus necessary expenses. Theoretically, it's the cash the company could return to shareholders as dividends if the company chose to grow no further. In its simplest form, free cash flow is found by taking operating cash flow and subtracting capital expenditures. Free cash flow is used to measure a company's profitability.

Earnings per Share (EPS): The company's net earnings divided by number of shares outstanding. It shows the value of earnings relative to each share of stock, which is a key measure of a stock's intrinsic value.

Where Our Story Begins

MANY OF MY LIFE'S STORIES involve the San Diego Convention Center.

Growing up, my father and I would make an annual pilgrimage to the modern building on the waterfront to enjoy the auto show and check out the latest models. In the early 1990s, before it exploded in popularity, the Comic-Con was a fun event to go to, rather than the giant media circus it has become today. It's even where my high school decided to locate our prom.

But our story starts much later than those events, at the end of 2008. At that time, at the San Diego Convention Center, I sat for the Chartered Financial Analyst (CFA) Level 1 Exam. It's a three-year self-study course, covering everything from accounting to ethics to economics to valuation metrics. The course material came in six large textbooks. A CFA designation is invaluable to employers, and 2008 was certainly a year employees needed to do something to look more valuable to an employer.

But it was also the year that the course material's content seemed out of whack with reality. To me, taking the exam was an exercise in cognitive dissonance, the idea that you're holding two different and contradictory ideas in your mind at the same time.

What had been going on throughout 2008—the financial crisis—was simply impossible according to the prevailing academic theories about how economies and stock valuation worked. But it was still the only thing that myself and the other test-takers could talk about during the break periods. (Markets wouldn't fully reach their bottom until March 2009, a few months later.)

For example, in October 2008, stocks moved so far outside their historical averages on a daily basis that they had three separate "six sigma" events. That's a statistical term for something that should happen about once every 1.5 million years. If it's happening three times in a month, then the conventional way of looking at risk in 2008 was certainly not holding up to reality.

What happened? The traditional world view of investing had failed . . . spectacularly so. This prevailing view, known as modern portfolio theory (MPT), is back in favor today as markets have calmed in the post–financial crisis universe.

But this theory is based on so many false assumptions that, like a broken clock, it can only periodically be correct out of sheer luck rather than anything else.

For instance, one part of the theory is that all investors know all pertinent information about a stock out there already. That's simply not the case. Another component is that investors are tax-efficient. Again, that doesn't always happen. Yet another maintains that all investors are risk averse. That can't explain why you'd invest in a different mix of assets as a retiree than you might if you were just getting started out investing and were looking to make a killing.

The list goes on.

The point isn't that the MPT theory is wrong; it's that it's been thoroughly debunked by the facts. At least, it should have been.

Again, the theory is back in favor with traders today, as though the 2008 market crash couldn't happen again. Or that the 1987 market crash, a one-day, 22 percent drop in stocks couldn't happen again. (Well, it can't, but only because exchanges put in "circuit breakers" to simply close up early if there is a big drop.)

As an investor, your knowledge needs to come from doing. Academic theories are fine, but at the end of the day, proven or otherwise, they're still theories. I'm more concerned with putting real money to work and seeing how a trade plays out.

The rest of this book is pretty simple. Each chapter is a case study from a real trade that I've made. It includes personal trades going back about 15 years, when I first started buying individual stocks instead of funds, and includes trades I've made across various newsletters I've written for as well. That includes services like *Insider Hotline*, the *Braintrust*, and *Crisis Point Investor*, my current newsletters, as well as other newsletters I've worked on in the past during my time at Newsmax. Since I tend to invest in most of the trades I make there, they're my babies too.

In each case study, I'll lay out what the rationale was for that investment, what happened, and how I adjusted the trade as events changed. Looking at these trades provides a much better way of explaining the failures of academic theory and coming up with a working alternative. If you're interested in that subject, refer to my 2013 book, *Uncharted: Your Guide to Investing in the Age of Uncertainty*.

Finally, I'll close out each chapter by running the trade post-mortem through a simple three-quality filter. The filter will show us how the trade was safe, debt-free, and enriching. Of course, not every trade hit all three criteria right away, and adjustments are needed. That fits in with the idea that the real world of investing can be a bit messier—but far more rewarding—than the modern portfolio theory crowd would have you believe.

By the end of this book, you should feel empowered to make similar decisions when facing a new (or existing) investment opportunity. You'll have plenty of real-world examples to draw on, not more academic theory. To some extent, this book is about how I made my first million or so. But on another deeper level, it's about how to look at every investment opportunity that comes your way and decide whether or not it's a worthy use of your capital and time.

And if you read through all the lows and highs of investing in individual stocks and options and decide that that isn't your style, in closing, I'll include a sample portfolio for passive investors who want to get great returns over time without having to continually trade the markets.

PART I

CORE TRADES

In this section, we'll be looking at what I call "core trades." These are investments where you can follow a buy-and-hold model, because here is where we invest in great companies with long-term advantages over competitors. It might be a better product, better market share, or a basket of powerful brands.

But we don't have to live with buy-and-hold returns with these investments. For many of these trades, shares may provide great long-term returns but will often trade sideways or out of favor with the rest of the market for a prolonged time. We'll look at how I've used options to boost returns on these trades to further improve their returns.

CHAPTER 1

Intel

*Building Big Profits in
"Brick-and-Mortar" Tech*

INVESTORS ARE FASCINATED WITH "THE next big thing." Everyone wants to find the next huge moneymaker—the next Wal-Mart or the next Microsoft—before it's a big, well-known company. Why? It's simple. In the process of going from a small company to a big company, share values multiply. Investing just a few thousand dollars in a small company that becomes the next big thing of its sector can create a millionaire in the process.

It's no surprise that the sector offering investors this opportunity is in technology. That's because technology is disruptive. A new gadget or app can explode in popularity overnight, upending the status quo that may have existed for months or years before.

But the land of technology is a graveyard as well. Many new promising technologies fail to pan out. Or consumers don't like the latest item. Or, in the rush to get a new product to market, a company skips necessary tests and the product is a dud—like Samsung's explosion-prone Note 7 phone, an item quickly shipped and quickly recalled in 2016.

But as an investor, you can play technology with less risk. That's because most technology relies on multiple suppliers to create a product. A smartphone may be manufactured by Samsung or Apple, but they don't create the whole product in-house. Teams at other companies put together the software and hardware parts that come together to make the whole thing work.

So while many investors are focused on some hot technology play, the best investments in the past few years have come from a different place instead—the old-school, brick-and-mortar tech companies still manufacturing physical products.

Case in point, consider **Intel (INTC)** back in 2013. At the time, the chipmaker was facing twin troubles. First was the notion of the "death of the PC." That was the belief that smartphones, tablets, and other technologies would replace the traditional personal computer. It was a belief based on surging sales for these new gadgets and slowing sales in PCs relative to these new gadgets.[1] The second trouble was a new technology investment theme: the cloud. This theme was simple. All your information would be stored in the cloud, and you could access all your files, anytime, anywhere, from any connected technology.

Let's unpack those ideas one by one. The personal computer, while ubiquitous, is still the best form of technology for productive work. With large screens and full keyboards, there's more functionality in a PC than in a tablet or smartphone. Those technologies are simply stopgaps.

What's more, since everyone who needed a PC owned one by the end of the 1990s, sales have been slowing. It's one thing to buy a first computer, but when it comes time to replace it with a newer model, the replacement times are staggered. Some do so every year or so, others might hold out a decade, until the old one finally falls apart.

Furthermore, despite the notion that the cloud was the next big thing, at the end of the day, the cloud was simply someone else's computer. It still needed all the traditional manufactured parts that a personal computer or other devices would, including memory, storage, processing power, and a means of interacting with wireless devices.

It seemed clear to me that the death-of-the-PC narrative that the market was swallowing might have been unduly pessimistic. At the same time, the cloud story was a narrative that was possibly too optimistic. But no matter how those stories panned out, we'd continue to see the market develop upgrades to existing devices and create new ones. Those devices would still require key parts. Companies like Intel could adapt to that changing market, as the company had done since the 1970s, when it was first founded.

So on August 22, 2013, I advised members of the *Braintrust* financial service to buy shares of Intel. At the time, shares traded at $22.23. The company had a great valuation, an above-average dividend yield and, more important, a growing dividend. Shares seemed undervalued given the death-of-the-PC narrative and given the company's primary focus in making processing chips for the PC market.

That proved to be the case. Shares of Intel started to move, making a sizeable rally to around $30 per share 10 months later. With shares up more than 35 percent in less than a year, a few opportunities were starting to emerge. Shares could have been sold immediately and invested elsewhere. But the narratives affecting Intel's share price were only beginning to change. Enthusiasm for investing in the cloud space was starting to wane, and fears of the decline of the PC industry were likewise fading quickly.

That's a common situation in investing, where some of the profits are made. When you invest when things look bad, all they have to do to get better is get "less bad." That can come from the start of better news, like improving earnings, or it can come from the simple fact that there's no new bad news that could come out and keep shares down and out.

Based on the sizeable rally in shares for the tech giant, I thought the best opportunity would be to sell covered calls on Intel shares rather than cash out quickly. By selling covered calls, there was an opportunity to make more money, and if shares rallied further, there'd be the chance to sell out at a bigger profit later. I selected the January 2015 $33 calls on the company, trading for $0.86, or $86 per contract.

While that didn't sound like much, it gave some more upside on the shares, and represented a cash payout close to the company's annual dividend payout. Essentially, the worst-case scenario was that I'd get paid double what the company was paying out to shareholders. It's hard to come up with a better win-win situation in the markets.

Shares of Intel ended up faring better than expected. They closed out January 2015 closer to $36 than $33, and the options were expired. But I'm not kicking myself for missing out on the maximum potential return on the trade. That's because, since then, shares of the company haven't gone too much higher than $36 and have even traded back below $30 on a few occasions as well.

In fact, in March 2015, after shares had made a pullback to around $30—a 20 percent drop from where I had been called away just two months before—I ended up selling the October 2015 $27 put option on Intel. I was betting that the company was no longer as out of favor with the market as it had been and that, as a result, shares would likely trade in a range in the $30s. Going back that far into the $20s would have been unduly pessimistic.

That proved to be the case, as this third trade in Intel expired worthless in October. I kept 100 percent of the $110 premium per contract that I sold as a result. So did subscribers of the *Braintrust* service, who were now becoming quite familiar with Intel after our various trades to profit from it.

This trade is what investing is about at its core. Finding an undervalued opportunity and letting it get near its true value. Whether you want to take profits and run or try to improve your returns with alternative strategies like using options can make a big difference, although it may mean being in the trade longer and passing up on other potential opportunities.

Even today, many of these traditional, old-school technology companies continue to make huge profits in areas that are out of favor with a tech crowd leaning more toward social media companies and other new feats. Whatever new technologies *do* develop, there will still be a need for the physical infrastructure that makes it possible. A mobile app is worthless if it can't be run on any smartphone. That's why companies like Intel can offer tremendous trading opportunities at the right price.

Let's run this series of trades through our three key investment criteria and see how we end up:

Safe: The trade seemed safe at the time of the initial investment. Shares were off on fears that the PC market, the primary source of Intel's revenue, would collapse. Yet at the same time, Intel would be able to profit by producing chips for other, newer devices like smartphones and tablets, which were soaring in popularity.

What's more, the chip space is a small market. Reputation matters. Intel was the trusted name for many chips, whereas other competitors had a tougher problem. It's bizarre to think that the market was substantially mispricing the stock in the first place, given its industry reputation and valuation. These all added up to a trade that looked incredibly high reward, low risk.

That safety was further compounded by the ability to use options to mitigate the risk. There may be times when it makes sense to just go out and buy shares, like back in 2013. But as shares rose, covered call writing seemed to strike the balance of protecting the gain while holding out for even better returns. And by 2015, with the company starting to show a new trading range, the best low-risk solution to stay safe was to sell put options, since shares had gotten substantially cheaper in a shorter amount of time, but weren't quite at a price where I'd want to buy them outright.

Debt-Free: This is the kind of trade where an investor could allocate a significant amount of their capital to the trade. As a global industry leader, investing in companies like Intel when they're out of favor is a no-brainer. But to improve solvency, I added the options trades. After all, following a big rally, shares would likely pause before going higher. Stocks make that kind of move all the time, even during tremendous bull markets. Using options to take some money out of the trade was a sensible and logical move.

Of course, I don't always expect to get called away on an options trade. On this specific trade, however, I did. That's OK. Getting out of the trade meant taking profits while the stock was still up. Given Intel's subsequent trading history, the returns could have been a lot lower at a later time (although shares still haven't dropped below the $22.23 entry price as I write).

Finally, by selling a put option against shares later on, I managed to generate some more income without having to put all that cash I had from the Intel sale back into shares right away. That kept cash on the sidelines to put to use in buying stocks that were now a bargain, which they weren't back in 2013 when Intel was starting to look like one.

Rich: Investing in the brick-and-mortar tech names isn't going to lead to gangbuster returns like it might have in the 1990s. Back then, the Internet revolution was so powerful because computers were finally becoming commonplace at every office workstation and even in every home. Now they're ubiquitous. But a trade like this does have the ability to create long-term wealth. These companies can and do trade out of favor with the markets. They're not the hot growth story they used to be, but they're steady players with a solid operating history that have gotten better with profitability, profit margins, and cash flow over time.

As a result, there's usually an opportunity in at least one of these tech names every year that could lead to gains of 50 percent or more. In the Intel trade, I made 58.58 percent on the underlying shares I had bought in 2013 in a year and a half. I made another $86 per 100 shares in the covered call that expired in early 2015. Later that year, as shares sold off a bit and had gotten cheaper—but not as cheaper as what I had originally paid—there was an opportunity to make another $110 per 100 shares by selling a put.

In total, I got about 10 percent of the original trade back in cash thanks to the options positions. That's not a bad return over two years in and of itself. Adding 5 percent to your returns every year above what the stock market is giving is a way to grow your wealth investing in quality companies like Intel without getting too aggressive in your investment picks.

CHAPTER 2

As Exciting as Watching Paint Dry

Investing in JM Smucker

INVESTING MAY SEEM TO COME down to two styles: growth and value. But it's often more complicated than that. It's really about where a company is at a given time. Sometimes a company trades like a growth stock, and sometimes it trades like a value stock. Operationally, a company may do the same thing as its shares. It may do well in one quarter but poorly the next.

It's better to think about companies in terms of how they perform operationally over time. There are generally two styles there as well: those that are steady, consistent performers and those whose operating performance swings wildly over time.

For most of your investment dollars, you'll be well off sticking to companies that have steady operations. For investments with bigger and faster profits but a higher chance of a reversal, the best money is made in companies that have uneven earnings and swing from big profits to big losses.

Companies that can produce steady and consistent quarterly earnings are rare but worth investing in for the bulk of your portfolio. These core investments fit the mold of a buy-and-hold investment that offers lower volatility than the overall market as well as solid dividend payments along the way—and, more import-ant, dividend payments that are likely to grow over time as the company continues to expand.

While these companies are worth making a major part of your portfolio, the opportunity to buy such a company at a great price is rare. Many opportunities will emerge during a market panic like the financial recession, but only a handful emerge in a normal year.

And once you do take the plunge and buy shares of steady per-formers, you'll want to sit back and ignore the position. It'll likely go nowhere for a long time before you start to notice the long-term uptrend.

One such opportunity that emerged was in **J. M. Smucker (SJM)**. The company is in the simple business of making jams and other preservatives. They bought Folgers Coffee a decade ago, making them a one-stop investment in the, well, breakfast space. As Folgers is the most popular brand in the home-brewed coffee space,[1] Smucker's is a clear winner.

Its profits and earnings definitely fall into the boring and con-sistent category. That's great for long-term shareholders, but it also means that investors tend to keep prices on the company at higher levels than the average stock.

Since the only real trick to buying steady performers is to wait for the right price, it can be a long wait for many investments.

However, on January 22, 2014, I put out an alert to members of my *Braintrust* investment service advising them to buy shares at or under $95.00. While, looking at a very long-term chart, shares were clearly going to continue up, there was some short-term weakness at work.

In the summer of 2013, shares were closing in on the $115 price point. I generally start to get interested in steady operators like J. M. Smucker after a 15 percent pullback, particularly given the market's optimism. Sales had been growing at a long-term rate of 7 percent per year, but had slowed in the most recent quarter. So instead, there was some temporary pessimism at work.

Smucker's shares didn't hit our buy price until February 3. At $95 per share, we had gotten around 18 percent below the stock's most recent peak.

While $95 looked like a good entry price, by the end of the month, shares were closing in on $91.00 and trading volume on the stock was surging. But I wasn't too worried given the company's dominance of the home coffee market, the jam market, and its long-term track record.

Indeed, late February proved to be the low point. Those who had been buying near the peak were finally crying uncle and letting stronger hands hold shares instead. Even at the $95 entry point, shares didn't look conventionally cheap. They traded at 15 times earnings. It was a discount from the 20 times earnings the S&P 500 was trading at the time, but it wasn't conventionally cheap.

Yet I've found over the years that 15 times earnings tends to be a good entry price for steady performers, particularly those in the consumer goods space. Those stocks tend to average closer to 20–25 times earnings when they're performing as expected. It's only when they have the occasional deviation that markets get unduly concerned. That was the case with Smucker's in early 2014 as we bought shares.

The trade quickly moved back into the profitable column. And there it sat for months on end, quietly earning us money while more exciting short-term trades came and went. It did exactly what it was supposed to do and was even paying us for the privilege of holding shares!

By October 2015, however, not only had shares gotten back to the old high, but they were on the verge of making new ones.

When a company is on the verge of making new highs, one of two things tends to happen. Either it powers through and makes a huge move, or it starts to drift downward again. For consumer goods companies with a steady operating history, the latter is usually the case. After all, it's a slow-growing long-term wealth-building opportunity, not a quick trade.

What's more, shares were now up more than 30 percent in less than 18 months. That's a sizeable move for any big, well-known company, even if it had a sizeable decline earlier. On October 14, 2015, I decided it was time to hedge the gain against a possible pullback in shares. I issued an alert to sell April 2016 $125 call options on the trade. Selling for $3.70, each contract was for $370—or about 4 percent of our original trade.

Come April, the options would either expire in-the-money or not. If they were in-the-money, we'd be out at $125 per share and keep our extra $370 per 100 shares. If not, we'd *still* keep the $370, but we'd also keep the shares and have the opportunity to sell in the future or sell more call options against the position. In short, this trade was now putting us into a win-win position.

When I sell call options against an open position, I'm usually at a point where I don't mind either outcome. I'll either lock in profits if the trade closes or create a bigger stream of income from selling options again and again. In April 2016, however, shares of J. M. Smucker traded over $125 and were subsequently called away. With dividends, the return on shares was 43.22 percent. With the additional $370 from selling the call option, the returns cleared 46 percent within 26 months of holding shares.

While many other stocks had bigger gains over that time, many also had bigger swings along the way. This was a low-risk trade at the price we bought and proved to be a sizeable winner in a short amount of time. Let's see the specifics of it as we take a look at this trade through the lens of our three criteria:

Safe: It's hard to call a trade safe when you're buying shares while they're declining. But that's how most successful investors enter into a trade, particularly if they have a long-term outlook in mind. A company that has fallen far enough from a recent peak, say 10 percent, may produce enough fear to encourage further selling. At a 20 percent discount from its peak, there's a relative bargain, particularly in a consumer goods stock like J. M. Smucker.

More important, given the company's industry position in coffee and preserves, it would still perform well operationally. Despite the recent slip in sales growth, the company's long-term record of sales growth was solid. This was a position that looked safer than it originally seemed at first glance.

There was also safety in the company's dividend payments, as well as the subsequent options trade. Regular cash payments to shareholders provide a flow of cash that can be reinvested, either in the same stock or in a new investment idea, or the cash can be used elsewhere. It means that even if shares were to trade sideways or down for a prolonged period of time, shareholders would still be rewarded with payments while waiting for a price recovery.

In short, the high likelihood of the business continuing to grow, coupled with the income opportunities, made it a low-risk, moderate-reward trade. It might not have had the same return as buying a hot stock on the cusp of a major upswing, but the odds of losing money were low. That's what I call a safe investment: one where your risk of losing money is as close to zero as possible.

Debt-Free: At $95.00 per share at entry, shares of Smucker's were expensive to buy into. A 100-share stake, the minimum to make call writing possible, would tally $9,500. That's a tall order for many investors. But it's not impossible.

But since the company fell into a category of safe over the long term, it was a prime candidate to be a core holding for any investor, even if such a large holding made the trade look more insolvent. As a core holding, it's OK to have a little more of your portfolio there than in a more trade-oriented investment. With companies that fit the criteria of steady earners, there's plenty of investor interest. That's why they tend to be pricier than the market most of the time.

So there's no trick to staying debt-free in a trade like this—as long as there's demand, you should be able to get out of the trade quickly and easily. But if you own a company that can consistently perform, you might not want to.

What about the role of covered call writing? It might seem that such an activity might make a position more insolvent. After all, now you have two positions to monitor: the stock and the affiliated options. And if you need to clear out quickly, it may be difficult without moving the price of the option substantially. But I've never had a problem closing out a trade before expiration, and I've only rarely had to do so. Sometimes I may "roll" an options position, where I buy back an option and then sell a new one with a longer time before expiration. Even in that situation, adding options trades clearly adds value. When you sell a covered call option, you're setting a price you're willing to sell at while things look rational, so you don't have to sell out at an inopportune moment. You're getting extra income out of a trade by selling calls. And if you sell options with strike dates 6–8 months out from your sale date, as I tend to do, the income from that option is usually close to or greater than an annual dividend payment. I view these as benefits that improve investment returns over time rather than make a trade potentially difficult to exit.

Rich: This is a classic trade to look at for how to build long-term wealth. Buying a temporarily out-of-favor company that was the leader in a small niche has proved to be profitable over the long haul. Sometimes, shares of such companies will be undervalued, like it was when I purchased shares in 2014. And sometimes shares will run a bit ahead of where the company is likely to go, as happened when I got called away from the position in early 2016.

This kind of trade involving a stock purchase, rally, and covered call writing activity can be endlessly repeated as a strategy, even with the same stock. As I write today, J. M. Smucker shares are once again nearing a 20 percent discount from a new all-time high—that high was $150 this time around and not $115.

It's no surprise that a company of J. M. Smucker's caliber can continue to make higher highs as time goes on. Over the very long term, investors might even find it better to wait for a pullback, buy, and then never do anything else like selling shares or covered call options. It may mean sitting through periodic declines, but over time, the rewards could outweigh the extra short-term profits from engaging in call writing.

CHAPTER 3

PacWest Bancorp

Fast Profits in an Unloved Sector

AS AN INVESTOR, I'M OFTEN thinking about where most traders are focused—and what corners of the market they're avoiding. Typically, there will be several shifts throughout a year.

But one area has remained out of favor for more than eight years as I write: the banks. Many investors have avoided the banks in the post–financial crisis world. I can't blame them. Many bank stocks fell 80 to 90 percent during that crisis and still haven't recovered, even as the market has roared to new highs. And that doesn't include the banks that went bankrupt or were merged with other banks at ultralow prices.[1]

It's no surprise that the sector remains out of favor even today. But an out-of-favor sector presents a tremendous opportunity if you know where to look.

Think about it this way: there are really two banking sectors. There are the big players who are part of what we call "Wall Street," and there are the smaller banks that we think of more as "Main Street." Most of the risk in our financial system is with the Wall Street banks. They're the ones that are part of the global financial system. They play the markets, help companies go public and finance operations, and otherwise make the big headlines.

But there are thousands of Main Street banks in the United States alone, and most of them don't engage in that kind of activity. Rather, they do what you expect from banks: they make loans to people and businesses in their community that they know. Think less *Wall Street* and more *It's a Wonderful Life*.

That's why these smaller, community banks look interesting from an investment standpoint. Because there's a bit of a stigma around the banking stocks in general, there's solid value in many banking stocks big and small alike. What's more, when there's fear in the markets, the banks tend to get some of the worst treatment—only to recover when the fear subsides.

Best of all, smaller banks are going the way of the dinosaur. The entire sector is getting gobbled up by the big names. The Wall Street term for this is *industry consolidation*. What it means is that of the 14,000 different banks in 1986, 30 years later, there are only 5,100, a loss of nearly two-thirds.[2] Yes, some of those banks went bankrupt. But most of those banks simply merged with bigger banks to create even bigger banks.

That's a trend likely to continue, and investing in smaller banks today is a way to enjoy a solid value, pick up a reasonable dividend payment, and possibly get a fat payout if there's a buyout offer. It's become easier, if not far cheaper, for a bank to simply buy a new client base rather than try to expand its operations one new client at a time.

Again, this all adds up to an interesting sector filled with everything from microcap companies to major global players. Even better have been the periodic bouts of fear in the markets that have plagued the bank stocks.

In early 2016, following the Federal Reserve's first interest rate hike in nine years, bank shares slid. That seems counterintuitive.

If interest rates rise, banks should be able to charge more interest on their loans. Consumers are now used to getting no or very little interest on their savings account, so payouts there can lag as rates rise. In theory, banks should be more profitable as rates rise. Yet bank stocks took a steep dive, bigger than the overall market correction that started off 2016.

Amid the carnage, I took the opportunity to buy shares of **PacWest Bancorp (PACW)** on February 9, 2016, at $32.42. It's a midcap bank based out of California, with 79 branches there and 1 in North Carolina. Earnings were solid thanks to rising real estate prices on the West Coast and the lack of energy loans that were plaguing other banks at the time.

The company traded at a mouthwatering 11.6 times earnings. But more important than earnings was the bank's valuation. It was trading at a discount to its book value. For a bank, book value is a conservative way of looking at the value of the bank relative to all its outstanding loans.

For instance, if a bank has a book value of $10 and is trading at $8 and the bank could liquidate itself in an orderly manner, there'd be $10 in cash against shares trading at $8. It's not quite free money, but it is a bargain hiding in plain sight.

Granted, PacWest only traded at a book value of 0.93, about a 7 percent discount to its total outstanding loans. But banks tend to trade at 1.2 to 1.3 book value, or a 20–30 percent *premium* to the value of their outstanding loans. Banks that get acquired tend to sell out at 1.5 to 2 times book value. So in the event that shares were picked up by a competitor, there could be huge upside to the trade. It also meant that, while bank shares could still decline further, we were safe from an operational and valuation standpoint.

Finally, amid the sell-off, corporate insiders were picking up shares. The CFO had picked up nearly $100,000 worth of shares in late 2015. The president and CEO joined the fray in late January by buying over $127,000 in shares. Directors were also picking up shares in the same period. These weren't executives exercising their options. These were purchases made on the open market with their own money. What did all these corporate insiders know that Mr. Market didn't? Probably that the bank had been unfairly beaten down and was now a value.

So it should be no surprise that the excellent value, high yield, and insider buying made it a prime investment opportunity not just for me but for subscribers of the *Insider Hotline* newsletter. We bought shares on February 9.

We exited the trade less than 10 weeks later, on April 19. What happened? Everything worked out quickly. The fear in the markets subsided. Stocks rose, and the bank stocks, which had been more heavily hit, rallied further as a result. In that period, we made a return of 23.75 percent as shares moved from the low $30s to around $40.

Earnings continued to come in, showing that the bank was still doing well from an operational standpoint, although shares were now trading above their book value. But insiders had started to take profits, and with the huge surge in share price, I felt that taking quick profits of more than 20 percent here would free up capital to put into new investment ideas that were starting to emerge.

After all, you don't go broke taking a profit. And since stocks return around 8 percent on average over time, getting three times that much in the space of a few weeks is the kind of opportunity that just can't be passed up.

Today, the community bank stocks still represent an area of perpetual interest. They had a solid rally in 2016, but are still an out-of-favor and unloved spot in the market, particularly smaller banks that might have made investments in the beaten-down energy space that now trade at an even bigger discount to their book value than PacWest did.

Here's how I see the trade unfolding through our three investment criteria:

Safe: While the bank stocks can be risky when fear perks up in the market, I felt the trade was safe for a few reasons. First, we were buying *during* that fear. Shares had dropped to the low $30s from the low $40s in the space of a few months. When you have a stock that's doing well operationally but has sold off twice as much as the market in the same time frame, you're likely to get market-beating returns when the situation turns around.

Second, we were buying at a discount to book value. Most banks trade at a premium on average, and smaller banks that get a buyout offer to become part of a bigger bank tend to trade at an even bigger premium as a result. But in this case, the company could have called in all its loans and the value would still be greater than what shares were paying at the time. And with a fat 5 percent dividend, it was clearly the kind of company where investors would be well paid to wait for things to change as they invariably do.

Third, we were buying into an out-of-favor sector. That meant that we were looking at buying a relative bargain in the market to begin with. But the banking sector is still unique. It's really two sectors that most investors think of as one. I was buying into the smaller, more traditional banks, not the bigger banks that had gotten into trouble during the financial crisis due to their willingness to forego loans to invest in derivatives and other fancy products instead. Loans and credit lines are easy to understand. Interest rate swaps and other exotic, complicated products aren't.

A local bank that's making loans and keeping those loans on their books is pretty easy to analyze. And there are still thousands of them out there, which makes it easy to find safe investment opportunities like PacWest.

Debt-free: We stayed out of financial danger on this trade by taking profits rather quickly once they emerged. While many investors might be tempted to hold on to a solid dividend-paying name, the banking sector remains jittery. That created the opportunity in the first place that allowed us to make the quick gain. But the paper gain could have become a loss had the market slipped back into fear mode, which can happen quickly where the banks are concerned.

Staying solvent and avoiding going into debt when investing means avoiding those big risks. Part of that isn't how the trade ends, but how it begins. We stayed financially safe on the trade from the get-go by waiting to invest in a company that was trading below book value, the measure of what the loans were worth. In some industries, book value is too conservative. A company might list an asset bought years ago that's now worth far more.

But bank loans are different. From the day the loan paperwork is signed, it's worth what it's worth. It can't become worth more. But a loan *can* lose its value should the borrower face cash-flow problems or have a problem with the underlying asset that's backing the loan. That's what happened with the financial crisis: millions of mortgages were backed by homes now worth substantially less than the outstanding loan amount.

In the post–financial crisis world, even with smaller banks that make traditional loans and don't get involved with Wall Street's antics, it's better to give yourself some wiggle room in case some of the loans go bad. That's why the discount to book value is so critical in this sector of the market.

Rich: The trade helped make us rich in a few ways. First, we got paid to wait with a generous dividend. During the 10 weeks it was held in *Insider Hotline*, we got a dividend of $0.50, or 1.5 percent of the $32.42 purchase price. That worked out closer to 6 percent annually, which would be a solid return even if the stock went nowhere.

But markets started turning up, and being in the overly despised banking sector meant bigger profits. At the end of a bear market, when the good and bad have been thrown out at once, Mr. Market tends to unduly reward those firms that have unduly suffered during the decline. That was the case here—with shares up nearly three times as much as the S&P 500 over the same period.

There's no secret to getting rich. You simply need to find what's out of favor now and what's likely to outperform once Mr. Market changes his mind. Given the fear that investors still have in the banking sector, this is one area ripe for further market-beating opportunities in the future.

CHAPTER 4

McDonald's and the Power of Yield on Cost

The Overlooked Secret to Superior Income Investments

MOST INVESTORS WITH AN EYE toward receiving an income tend to focus on a stock's dividend yield. That's a reasonable starting point. After all, the yield tells you what to expect if you own shares for a year. Right now, the average yield on the S&P 500 Index is about 2.12 percent. In other words, for every $100 you invested in the market as a whole, you could expect $2.12 in income each year.

Again, it's a reasonable starting point. But it's a static starting point. Companies change their yields all the time. Some companies may need to cut their dividends, like many energy stocks have done in the past few years as oil prices fell 70 percent from their peak. Many financial companies likewise cut or eliminated their dividends entirely during the financial crisis. That was a crushing blow, since many of the big banks were yielding in the 3–5 percent range.

That's the bad news about looking at current yield—it may not reflect the future. But likewise, a company that raises its dividends over time may end up being an even better income play. What's more, as companies raise their dividends, provided the market believes it's a sustainable increase, share prices tend to rise as well.

Imagine buying a stock at $100 with an annual payment of $2. The yield is 2 percent. Say the company doubles the dividend to $4. Chances are the price will rise as well because of the higher payout. After all, investors were buying the stock with a 2 percent dividend, and at $100, it would now be 4 percent. That's why share prices tend to rise with dividend increases, all other things being equal (i.e., the company still has to be growing its earnings fast enough to be able to pay out the increased dividends to shareholders).

That means if you bought at $100 and you were now earning $4 in dividends, your yield would be 4 percent of what you originally payed. This is known as your "yield on cost," and it's one of investing's greatest assets that can work in your favor.

The premise of yield on cost is simple. It's how much of your *original* stake you're getting out of your capital each year. Investing in companies with a history of dividend increases means that you'll be getting an increasingly higher yield on cost as time goes on, irrespective of how the share price performs.

My experience discovering the power of yield on cost started in 2003. In that year, an S&P 500 company with a long history of paying higher dividends found itself facing a short-term problem: it had finally recorded its first losing quarter in the company's history. The company had previously warned that its earnings were in danger of being near a loss seven times before—but it was the eighth time that it finally happened.

That company was **McDonald's (MCD)**. It was facing a lot of issues that many large businesses face: same-store sales were declining, and restructuring the business was proving to be more difficult than expected. Even worse, the company had tried to turn things around with a $1 Big Mac promotion, but the costs of advertising, making, and packing the burger meant a loss of $0.07–0.08 for each sale.[1] In other words, they lost a little money on each one, but they made up for it on the volume.

Shares sank by double-digits to multiyear lows below $17.00. Investors fled the company in droves, seeing the kind of danger they saw in other restaurants having problems at the time. For instance, the Planet Hollywood chain had recently gone out of business as well.[2]

This is exactly the kind of "problem" an investor should love to find. It's clear that McDonald's problems were the result of some short-term decisions that weren't working out so well but also that things would eventually turn themselves around. The company didn't have the same problems as fad restaurant chains, and fears of bankruptcy were still high in 2002 following the dot-com crash. As a result, the subsequent rise in McDonald's shares—and improving outlook—should have come as no surprise to investors.

I'd like to say that I bought shares in 2003. But I didn't. I came close to it, but as a result of my limited capital, I wanted to focus on the best opportunities at the time. In the early 2000s, the start of a powerful rally in commodities and real estate investments was just beginning, and that's where the bigger gains were (as we'll see in the next section).

But in 2009, I did end up buying shares of McDonald's. The price was higher, but a few things had changed. Personally, I had a lot of cash on the sidelines to put to work following my sale of now-overpriced commodity stocks. What's more, the fallout from the financial crisis put a lot of powerful brands like McDonald's on sale. Unlike the profitable-today, declining-tomorrow rough-and-tumble of investing in the commodity space, I know this is a position that will continue to reward me for decades to come.

Finally, McDonald's was doing great operationally. Out of 30 stocks in the Dow Jones Industrial Average, only McDonald's and Wal-Mart (WMT) ended 2008 higher than what the year started. The company was holding up well in what would prove to be the biggest recession since the Great Depression.[3] Buying in 2009, shares were a modest bargain thanks to the market sell-off in 2008. But the company wasn't as great a bargain in 2003, when there was a lot more uncertainty surrounding its operations and profitability.

That's OK, because even buying at that later date, I've now been enjoying seven years of growing dividends. And with it, a rising share price. That leads to the most important aspect of investing in a company like McDonald's: having the patience to get a fantastic yield on cost.

Yield on cost is a great tool for managing your existing portfolio positions. When you think about replacing a stock that offers a high yield on cost, you'll need to think about how you're going to replace that income. It might look good on paper to replace a stock you own that currently yields 3 percent for a similar competing firm that yields 4 percent. But if your yield on cost is higher than 4 percent and if the competing firm isn't as good about raising dividends over time, the issue suddenly looks more complicated and realistic.

It would be absurd to sell McDonald's shares today if you had bought back in 2002 at $17 near the panic-low. The company's current payout of $3.76 is 3.35 percent at today's prices. But at $17, you're getting back a whopping 22.11 percent of your original capital every year—and the company's history of boosting the dividend means that your yield on cost will likely rise indefinitely. Even if you held off and bought shares after the financial crisis in 2009, at a price of around, say $55, then your yield on cost would still be 6.8 percent. If you can find a new investment that's going to have a higher yield on cost within a few years, that might be a reasonable trade-off. Good luck finding such an opportunity. That's an exceptionally tall order.

An investor with a great yield on cost looking to cash out could try to find a company with a higher yield and faster dividend growth. That's a riskier bet, since companies with high dividends tend to grow them more slowly. And companies with fast dividend growth in some years are offset by declines in others.

In theory, after owning a company long enough, you could be getting back a majority of your original stake every year, or even all of it. Say you bought shares of another company trading at a cheap valuation in the 2002 post-dot-com era, Apple (AAPL). A one-share stake in 2002 would pay $15.96 today (after adjusting for a recent seven-for-one split). But at the panic low, before the company even paid a dividend, shares traded as low as $9.00.

Of course, this is an extreme example, and it doesn't even look at Apple's phenomenal capital gains over the same time frame. But just looking at shares in terms of yield on cost, the 2003 investor is getting 168 percent of their original stake back every year. Of course, the shares would have to trade far higher as well!

That's the power of yield on cost. It's what makes some companies still worth buying and holding today.

And the best part is, companies with growing dividends that provide an increasing yield on cost over time lead to other opportunities as well. Between 2012 and 2015, McDonald's traded in a range between $80 and $100 per year. The dividend was still going up, and the company was still doing fine operationally. But you could have increased your returns every year selling covered calls on shares when they closed in on $100, grabbing enough income equivalent to double dividend payments over time. That's the strategy I used while holding shares. And when they got oversold down near $80, it also paid to sell put options, betting that the decline was over and that if it wasn't, I could get paid well for the "risk" of buying shares at $75.

I don't think it's too late to buy McDonald's shares, especially if you have a very long-term outlook in mind. While it's the kind of company you could ignore for 10 years easily, you could also take advantage of periodic slow-moving or underperforming periods to use options to make more money. But McDonald's isn't alone. Many other companies with a history of growing their dividends over time can provide a great yield on cost to fuel your future income needs.

A simple place to start is with a list of "dividend aristocrats." These are companies with a 25-year record of raising dividends. They're not all restaurants or consumer goods plays. While you'll find companies like Procter & Gamble (PG) and Colgate-Palmolive (CL), many industrial names like Emerson Electric (EMR) and Illinois Tool Works (ITW) fit the bill. So do insurance companies like Chubb (CB) and Cincinnati Financial (CINF).

While all these companies have modest dividend payouts, these specific companies have raised their dividends at least once annually over the past 50 years. Even McDonald's has been a dividend aristocrat for only 39 years!

While past performance is no indication of future performance, these companies are well-established and are the best of breed in their respective sectors. Since your investment lifetime is likely going to be 50 years, from your first job's 401(k) plan to the end of retirement, investing early in companies like these can lead to a massive yield on cost. This is where time is on your side.

Many technology companies aren't dividend aristocrats, simply because they haven't been around that long. But many older, established tech companies like Cisco (CSCO), Intel (INTC), and Microsoft (MSFT) have been great about establishing and raising dividends over time. I have no doubt that these companies will also become dividend aristocrats over time. Like McDonald's, their best days of growth may be behind them, but they still generate huge amounts of cash that can be returned to shareholders. As they do so with increasing amounts, their share prices will likely rise as well. In fact, in late 2016, Microsoft shares finally rose above their year-2000 tech bubble peak price.

Let's take a quick look at how McDonald's—and the underlying yield-on-cost rationale—fits into our world of finding safe, debt-free, and enriching investments:

Safe: McDonald's was absolutely a safe investment in 2009, being one of the few companies to go through the 2008 ringer without taking a major hit. In 2003, the company was arguably even safer, following the huge drop in shares as the company reported its first-ever quarterly loss. While the restaurant space in general is subject to fads and whims, McDonald's is one of the steadier plays in the industry.

Debt-Free: McDonald's meets this criterion handily. Despite the occasional slowdown in sales, the company faces little bankruptcy risk. While the company may disappoint investors with earnings, the company's large and international presence makes bankruptcy unlikely. Indeed, when looking at the restaurant sector as a whole, McDonald's offers the largest global presence.

The company's status as a dividend-growth champion also means investors can stay out of financial trouble while holding shares as well. They'll receive growing income out of the investment over time. What's more, a rising dividend tends to lift shares of a company as well over time, creating an upward spiral of wealth creation.

Rich: Like the tortoise and the hare, this is a case where slow and steady will win the race. And that's not just with McDonald's specifically but with a yield-on-cost investment strategy in general. A growing income tends to lead to higher stock prices, creating a virtuous cycle.

For companies whose shares periodically stay flat or fall during periods of dividend growth, you can add to your wealth with covered call writing strategies (or put-selling strategies to get paid for the risk of buying more should prices warrant). McDonald's will continue to reward investors far into the future, even though its days as a fast-growing company are long behind it.

CHAPTER 5

Investing in Insurance Companies

*Safe, Consistent, and Boring Profits in
This Heavily Regulated Industry*

THERE'S ONLY ONE INDUSTRY WHERE I'd be comfortable investing *all* my money. Sure, I enjoy picking through values wherever they are, but there's one sector that's regulated for profits but doesn't have to deal with infrastructure like a utility or telecom company. It's one that's been a big winner over time, although you wouldn't necessarily know it from the sector's slow daily trading.

I'm talking about the insurance sector. Insurance is a boring industry. That's a blessing, and probably one if its greatest assets right now. There's no single "hot" story here. The products aren't exactly innovative. In fact, many insurance companies exist to service a need that's often required by law.

The purpose of insurance is simple: you're looking to mitigate a potential risk that you might not be able to shoulder on your own. The loss of a home isn't something you can likely absorb—it's simply too big of an expense.

For most people, the same holds true with a car if it's damaged or stolen. Insurance companies simply pool a variety of different people looking to offset the same risk. And risk management is where well-run insurance firms do outstanding work.

Chances are your insurance company, thanks to intimate knowledge of its area of expertise and an army of actuaries, has a much better understanding of your specific risk needs than you ever will. Why? Because that's where they really earn their money. They receive premiums from you and, in exchange, pay out claims when losses occur.

In practice, insurance companies generally receive more in premiums than they have to pay out on any one policy. If they manage their risks right, they'll make a profit every year, barring some kind of large disaster like a hurricane or an earthquake. For some types of policies, like term life insurance (which is only for a set term) or car insurance, a company might never have to pay a claim.

For example, if you're a fortunate and never get in an accident or have a tree fall on your car or have your car stolen, your automobile insurance company will never lose money from having to pay out claims to you. You'll still have to pay them year after year, as required by law, to insure the car against the possibility of those events, of course.

With the rapid depreciating value of automobiles, chances are that by the time you do have a claim on a car, the money you receive from an insurance claim will be substantially below the initial value of the car. Therefore, rates are generally set according to the value of the asset being insured.

Here's the kicker, though: since the insurance company doesn't have to pay out the premiums it's been receiving from you right away (or potentially have to pay out on a policy ever), it can invest the insurance premium money in the meantime.

Even better, remember that it's not technically the company's money. That premium money by and large becomes a reserve pool for paying out claims. So on the balance sheet of an insurance company, its reserves are listed as a liability. But in reality, it can be a powerful asset. This money is known as "float." If the insurance company invests its float wisely, it makes money off other people's money. This powerful tool is the one used by Warren Buffett to grow the wealth of **Berkshire Hathaway (BRK-A)** over time. The insurance division of Berkshire has gone from having $20 million in float in 1965 to over $55 billion today. Indeed, as Buffett himself has said, "Float has cost us nothing, and in fact has made us money. Therein lies an accounting irony: Though our float is shown on our balance sheet as a liability, it has had a value to Berkshire greater than an equal amount of net worth would have had."[1]

Of course, float, like any other form of other people's money, can go the other way. **American Insurance Group (AIG)** invested a substantial amount of its float in credit default swaps, subprime mortgages, and other investments that caused the company to go crawling for a government bailout in 2008. Prudent management is key.

So why can insurance work in a time of rising interest rates? Because for most insurance companies, their "float" is invested in safe assets like Treasury bills, notes, corporate bonds, and the like. Yes, higher rates mean their existing portfolio will take a hit in price. But the higher interest gained as a result could improve short-term results that traders tend to look for.

With the idea of higher interest rates in mind, as well as the safety of the insurance sector as a whole, on August 22, 2013, I bought shares of **Cincinnati Financial (CINF)** after advising members of the *Braintrust* financial service to do the same. Our buy price was $47.16 per share.

Why Cincinnati Financial over other peers in the insurance space?

CINF offers property/casualty and life insurance. They're the 20th largest insurance company by market share in the United States. Their largest markets are in Ohio, Illinois, and Indiana, although they have operations in 39 states.

Cincinnati had a 3.3 percent dividend yield, a bit richer than other property and casualty insurance companies. More important, at the time, it had been raising the dividend for the past 53 years. Only nine other US companies can match that record.

Over the course of the year before we bought shares, their property/casualty premiums had risen 15 percent, in part due to higher prices on the renewal side. But here's the kicker: their combined ratio was 91.2 percent, compared to an industry average around 94 percent. The combined ratio measures the claims ratio versus the expense ratio. An insurance company with a ratio below 100 percent is making an underwriting profit.

In other words, even if they had no float to invest, they'd still be making money. Simply put, they were paying out less money in claims than they were receiving from premiums. Typically, the combined ratio is the insurance industry's go-to measure of a company's profitability. But like many other insurance stocks, CINF was pretty cheap compared to the overall market too. It traded at less than 15 times earnings, sported a profit margin of 13.2 percent, and had seen a surge in quarterly earnings growth year over year.

Yes, it had been cheaper, as was the case with many insurance stocks back in mid-2013. But a key nonfinancial indicator had popped up suggesting the stock remains cheap: insiders had turned slightly bullish. Besides the usual array of corporate officers and directors receiving and cashing stock options, a few officers had been buying shares on the open market. One officer had purchased 3,000 shares around the current price as recently as

July 29, 2013. Another open purchase came around June 7, 2013. More important to me as an investor, there had been no share sales by insiders within the two years prior.

Insider buying, especially in the absence of selling, is a good sign for investors. When corporate insiders are bullish on the prospects of their company to the point where they're putting outside money into the stock, they're sending a signal that they expect higher prices. Insiders owned about 9 percent of the company. That's far more than the average insider ownership of an S&P 500 company, and it's also large enough stake to ensure that shareholder interests and management interests are aligned.

Nevertheless, the combination of valuation, insider buying, and the safety of the insurance sector made the investment look like a terrific value. In hindsight, it proved to be a no-brainer investment.

After buying shares, we didn't do anything for more than two years. Shares gradually trended higher, but at such a slow pace that there was hardly any noticeable move on a daily basis. When the broad market swung higher, so did shares. When the broad market started pricing in fear, so did shares. But over time, share gradually clawed their way to higher returns than the broad market.

By early 2016, the trend had shifted. Shares were soaring, and at a time when the overall market was in decline. In late 2015, after the Federal Reserve had raised interest rates for the first time since the financial crisis, investors took money out of risky stocks and into safe dividend names. While the effect was most pronounced in the utility and telecom sector, the insurance industry was also attracting a lot of cash, pushing shares higher.

It was a trend that could continue, but also a sign that the easy money had been made. A bigger move up now would carry a higher risk of shares pulling back and losing those gains. I'd rather lock in those gains. So I advised members of the *Braintrust* to sell September 2016 $65 calls on February 10, 2016. Those calls allowed us to collect an extra $2.20 off the trade.

We ended up getting called away in September, as optimism in the insurance space carried shares even higher than their early 2016 surge. The trade was officially closed on September 9, 2016. With dividends, capital gains and the option premium, we had made 55.6 percent in just over three years. That's fantastic for a trade that was essentially flat the first year we held it and only started to take off in the latter half of 2015. What's more, over the same period, the S&P 500 Index returned roughly half as much as Cincinnati Financial.

Let's run this trade through our three filters and see how things played out:

Safe: This trade looked safe on a variety of levels. The valuation was good, even within the insurance space. Generally, insurers trade with a lower valuation than the broad market. After all, they're not tech stocks. They're in a highly regulated business with state and federal requirements for creating valid insurance contracts. That makes the overall sector a great place to invest. But there was also a bit of a discount here, even compared to other property/casualty insurers.

Furthermore, corporate insiders were also bullish. I love seeing a company's executives pick up shares of the firm they know best. It's a strong vote of confidence, particularly when multiple insiders are buying and none are selling, as occurred with Cincinnati Financial in mid-2013.

Finally, the company had a great long-term track record. While that's not necessarily an indication that *future* performance will be better, a company that can pay out increasing dividends for more than 50 years is likely being managed very conservatively and unlikely to take on a lot of risks. In investing, a lack of risk translates to the nebulous concept of safety.

Debt-Free: Insurance companies are generally not going to do anything too risky. Sure, there's a possibility that something will go wrong and that they'll make systematic investment mistakes with their float, as AIG did during the financial crisis. But that was *very* much the exception. Cincinnati Financial was in a different boat. Their investment float was invested in well-known assets and not risky, newer, and less understandable "assets" that popped up during the bubble years.

As an investment, the trade proved great to those holding shares as well. That's because shares paid a generous quarterly dividend, which was increased several times while we held shares. We also took advantage of a surge in shares to sell a covered call against our position, to further increase our income on the trade. Being able to take cash out of a trade ensures that, even if shares later face some challenges, we'll still get a lot of original capital out of the trade.

Rich: The numbers speak for themselves. While a 55.6 percent gain over three years might not sound phenomenal, it was a great return relative to the overall stock market during that time. That's because the market made new highs, suffered a 10 percent or so pullback, and gradually came back higher on three occasions during this period. While CINF didn't do much its first year of trading, it started to take off in late 2015. It became a market-beater shortly thereafter and didn't look back as shares really started to outperform the S&P 500.

The road to riches is sometimes slow and sometimes fast, particularly when investing in a large-cap name that might trade sideways for a long time before trending higher. This was a trade that took a long time, but rewarded us for having patience.

CHAPTER 6

Seagate Limited

Turning a Big Market Overreaction into Big Profits

MARKETS SEEM LIKE THEY GET things right. After all, as soon as new information about a company becomes publicly available, the price immediately shifts to account for that information. That's the basis of an academic theory about investing called the *efficient market theory* (EMT).

But while markets are mostly efficient most of the time, they do get it wrong. Finding and exploiting those opportunities is how you get fantastic market-beating returns time and again.

For instance, in May 2016, I picked up shares of **Seagate Limited (STX)** at $20.15 per share, after alerting members of *both Insider Hotline* and the *Braintrust* to this emerging opportunity.

It's easy in hindsight to state it so plainly. But at the time, buying those shares looked like the proverbial attempt to "catch a falling knife." That's because shares were on their way down, and seemed likely to continue doing so for the foreseeable future.

But that was just the market being inefficient and getting ahead of the facts. The facts were simple: Based out of Ireland, Seagate manufactures electronic data storage devices, from hard disk drives (HDD's) inside a computer to external storage. Chances are pretty good that if you have an external hard drive to back up your personal data, it's a Seagate product. They have about 44 percent of the market, in line with competitor **Western Digital (WDC)**.

In other words, Seagate was (and still is) tied for first place in a virtual duopoly. An industry that only has two players doesn't leave customers much leeway in terms of where to do business. In turn, that should mean higher profit margins than in more competitive industries.

And while Seagate was profitable, Mr. Market didn't like their most recent earnings. The company had reported about a month back that sales would be $2.6 billion instead of analyst expectations of $2.7 billion. Seriously, that was it. And somehow that was enough to send shares down more than 20 percent following earnings.

Do the math. That's only a 4 percent drop in sales, but given how sensitive traders have been to companies reporting weakness, it led to a sharp decline in the stock. After trading as high as $58.98 in the past year, the shares had lost nearly two thirds of their value and were now trading around $20.

Over the same time period, the S&P 500 had been flat overall, meaning that Seagate shares had underperformed the S&P 500 by 64.5 percent. Again, this was still a profitable company in a duopoly that had just had a modest decline in sales in one quarter!

But this wasn't just a trade on the relative performance of the shares. The sell-off had been so steep and quick that Seagate was now a value play.

By the time we bought, shares of Seagate traded at a forward P/E ratio of 9, against 22 times earnings for the average S&P 500 stock. The EV/EBITDA ratio stood at 4.99. When I worked in private equity, any EV/EBITDA ratio under 10 was considered cheap. That implies that Seagate could double and still have plenty of upside, even if the earnings drop proved to represent a permanent decline in sales rather than a one-time event.

But that's not all. Even after its sales decline, Seagate was still earning an impressive 22.6 percent return on equity. The balance sheet had leverage of 0.33, or $1 in debt for every $3 in assets. They weren't some overleveraged tech company that needed massive sales growth to survive. They were doing extremely well.

In fact, thanks to the severity of the recent sell-off amid the company's continued profitability, it was an amazing income play. The yield at the time we bought was a fantastically large 11.58 percent.

Like many other "brick-and-mortar" tech companies that make the tangible items needed to connect to the Internet, the valuation is excellent relative to the overall market. Although I started investing directly in stocks in the late 1990s, I didn't even touch a tech stock until after the financial crisis. When I did, it was in many of the brick-and-mortar plays that were too cheap to lose money on over time.

Even though such companies are generally out of favor with the market, they've held up well operationally, earning massive amounts of cash flow that don't need to be perpetually reinvested in the business, like many of today's tech start-up darlings. Seagate seemed like a worthy addition to the mix.

It should be no surprise that this turned out to be one of the big winners of 2016. What happened? The fear subsided and the facts won out, as they usually do in the end. The company's drop in sales proved to be a one-time affair, and sentiment in the hard drive space has been less pessimistic as sales have stopped declining.

For members of *Insider Hotline*, we simply sold out to make a sizeable profit in November 2016 as shares closed in on $40. From the low point shares had traded at, in the teens, shares had more than doubled.

For the *Braintrust*, where the trades get a little more complex, we sold October $34 calls on July 27. That added an additional $1.41

in income to our returns. Those options were exercised. Within a five-month span, we had made 77.04 percent return based on our original buy price.

Our timing was close to the bottom in the trade. While shares had dipped a little lower, they surged much higher within a few weeks as the company came out and reported earnings again. This time, because analysts had set the bar so low, the company had no problem beating expectations. And with the continued profitability of the firm and the dividend payouts firmly in place, investors started flocking to shares once again.

At its core, this trade was simple. The market got it severely wrong. And they had done it before, back when there was too much optimism in shares and they traded much higher. But after losing nearly two-thirds of their value in nearly a year, shares were trading as though bankruptcy was just around the corner. Yet, oddly, the company had the financial power to pay investors double-digit returns on their money just to own shares. Something had to give, and it should be no surprise that it broke in favor of shareholders.

The speed and severity of that change, however, even took me by surprise. I figured on some modest capital gains going forward of around 10–15 percent based on how oversold shares had gotten. Combined with the double-digit dividend, we would still be looking at a great return. But shares surged so far, so quickly, that there was then a bigger risk of another decline in shares.

Many stocks in long-term downtrends can have powerful counterrallies, and this could have been one of them. As I write, that doesn't seem to have been the case, but a slowdown in the economy or another poor quarterly earnings report from Seagate could lead to another big drop—and another great buying opportunity.

The principle of buying such a heavily out-of-favor, high-yielding stock is one to keep in mind. A few such opportunities emerge every year out of the markets, although not always in the brick-and-mortar technology world.

Here's how this market-trouncing trade looked through our three investment criteria:

Safe: On the surface, the trade didn't look safe. You could have pulled up a chart going back two years, when the stock traded as high as $70, and seen a huge downtrend. What made this time different? The facts. The company was still profitable. A mere 4 percent drop in sales didn't necessarily mean a downtrend. Many companies have fluctuating sales, earnings, and the like. There was no general trend here, and it could have easily been a one-time event.

Thanks to the sell-off, there was safety in holding shares. The hefty dividend meant that I would be well paid to wait and see what would unfold next. That made owning shares look like a far better bet than, say, making an options trade like selling put options or buying a call option and hoping for the best.

As the trade unfolded and shares had a massive rally, the safety in holding shares started to diminish. The market has been pricing brick-and-mortar technology names at a discount to other sectors, which meant, at least in the short term, that upside would be limited to maybe a double. As we closed in on that level, I found it prudent to simply take some of the risk off of the table, either by selling shares or by writing covered calls against shares as the situation warranted.

In either event, it also meant being out of the trade within the span of a few months with a 77 percent return. Over the same time period, the S&P 500 had gyrated a bit but was only up about 2 percent. That's the kind of relative return that can happen when you find out-of-favor names. That's the power of waiting for a sizeable margin of safety.

Debt-free: Part of staying debt-free, in my mind, includes getting a return of capital. If you can get cash out of a position and still own shares, you're becoming better off over time. That can come from dividends or covered call writing, or it can come from spinoffs or new shares that can be sold. Mostly, solvency means not overinvesting in a company to the point that getting out of your entire position is going to be a problem. As a large company, Seagate had no such problem.

When I bought shares of Seagate, the highest likelihood of a solid return on capital was from the massive dividend. At the time, the market priced Seagate Limited with a double-digit yield. Usually, that's a sign that traders expect a dividend cut.

But a quick look at the balance sheet showed that the company had a very low debt level. They also had great cash flow, even with declining sales. It was clear that they could continue to pay out a high yield.

The downside to such a large current yield is that it isn't likely to grow much over time. So I didn't see Seagate as a dividend-growth trade, which usually makes for a great Core Investment. But at the time, unless things were worse than expected, the high current yield and depressed share price made for a fantastic opportunity, as subsequent events proved.

Rich: This is a classic "how to get rich" trade. That's because we started with market fear that was short term in nature. Traders overreacted to the company's quarterly numbers. It proved to be a one-time event. And as I write, sales are modestly up. The worst of the sales decline seems to be behind us.

This trade shows the importance of looking beyond the headlines—like a company's quarterly earnings. Traders had assigned the wrong narrative to shares. Citing the rise of cloud computing and the death of the PC, it seemed that memory storage devices would be on their way out. Yet if anything, memory storage needs have exploded as people want to have more audio and video files. That's something that was unthought of 20 years ago, when most computer users were focused on smaller files like text documents.

Markets get trends wrong periodically over the short term. They're generally right over the long term, but they'll make mistakes along the way—like the tech bubble of the late 1990s. Watching the market for individual names making new multiyear lows can whittle down the investment world into a few heavily oversold companies that might have a chance of bouncing back. Out of the companies that make such a move, the next move is to find the ones that are still showing signs of huge profitability, even if they're out of favor now.

As for *staying* rich, it's important not to overstay your welcome. When I bought shares of Seagate at $20, it seemed likely that they'd eventually get back to $40. It seemed unlikely that they'd get back to the overoptimistic price level of $70 that they had traded at their peak any time in the foreseeable future. That's why I felt it best to take the profits earlier rather than later. It hit the return goals, just within a shorter amount of time than expected. That's how it goes with investing. Sometimes the wait'll be longer, sometimes it'll be shorter.

PART II

COMMODITY TRADES

While core trades should make up the bulk of your investment portfolio, their returns only start to look great over time. Over shorter periods, you can make fantastic, market-beating returns by investing in other areas, such as the more cyclical commodity market. It's an area all investors should be aware of, and it's one of the few places where investors can get big short-term returns without necessarily taking on substantial amounts of risk.

The case studies in this section illustrate the power of investing in commodities under a variety of circumstances—starting with my own personal story of how I got started investing—and going through what to look for in a commodity investment and when to strategically trade the commodity markets using tools like options.

CHAPTER 7

Silver
An Investment Start as Good as Gold

MY INVESTMENT JOURNEY STARTED IN childhood. That's proven fortunate. The sooner you start, the sooner you start to see the benefits of investing. Soon is a relative term though—even after investing for more than two decades, I'm just now starting to see the benefits of compounding. That's the name of the process where money makes money for you . . . and then that money makes even more money, and so on.

With the benefit of my knowledge today, there are a few things I'd do differently. But I wouldn't change my first "investment" of buying silver.

Technically, I didn't buy silver outright. Instead, I found a way to acquire silver at a low cost, although it involved a little bit of labor in the process.

What I did was go to a bank with cash, get as much coinage as possible, and try to find pre-1964 coins that contained 90 percent silver content. Starting at the age of six or seven, it was the perfect way to start building my wealth. It's a time-consuming process, but one that showed immediate benefits, even in the late 1980s and early 1990s, when silver traded around $4–7 an ounce at best.

Even at those prices, finding a silver quarter was a great find. It meant acquiring $1 or so in silver, but only paying $0.25 to do so. The math made sense. The amount of time going into it didn't always. As I grew up, I turned it into a business.

In the days before Coinstar machines at grocery stores could take your change, I'd offer to go through people's accumulated coinage, take it to the bank, and give them cash. It was a great first business, and I was able to make some paper money on top of all the silver coins that I was able to find.

When you have neighbors who have been saving up change for decades, you can find a lot of old coins. More important, I learned a valuable lesson about banks. When you bring in a suitcase full of change to a bank branch for a clerk to sort through, you're probably not going to be welcome there again for a while!

As a result of this work, I saw the opportunities that could open up with investing. I also realized that there were better ways to make money with less work—which in turn led me to stocks. But as a result of investing in silver, I also gravitated toward commodity-based stocks as well. Buying those stocks at the right time and catching an upswing can create far better returns than buying and holding the commodity itself. When silver prices were exploding in early 2011, silver stocks were making triple-digit returns!

Looking at my silver holdings over the past 25 years, there's been a lot going on. The metal has traded as low as $4 per ounce, but as high as $48 during the 2011 mania. As I write today, it's around $16, and could trend higher if inflation picks up. As I've gotten wealthier, however, I've found that physical gold is a better buy as it takes up far less space. Unfortunately, there's no way of finding gold in the coin rolls at your local bank!

By paying a dime for a silver dime, far below the spot price of silver even back in the days when it was $5 per ounce, it's nearly impossible to lose money on the trade. As investors, only a few opportunities will emerge over time that offer high upside and little to no downside. Those opportunities should be heavily bought and held until the opposite is true: there's little to no upside left and a high possibility of a big downside.

Unlike most of the other trades in this book, this is one that I haven't closed out yet. That's because I view precious metals more as a permanent core holding rather than a trade. Why? For the same reason that I pay for insurance on my car, home, and life. There are a lot of unknowns out there, and precious metals can help alleviate some of those worst unknown events.

Even today, I believe that every investor should own some physical gold and silver. It provides a valuable hedge against unexpected inflation or political uncertainty. With inflation expectations near zero, I could easily see the metal surging higher for that reason. And political uncertainty seemed to be the dominant headlines of 2016—and will likely continue as more elections around the world unfold in 2017, which could shake institutions like the European Union.

A word of caution though: I wouldn't go too far in the direction of precious metals. They have big up years and down years, and tend to just barely beat inflation over very long periods of time. An ounce of gold could buy the finest in men's fashion in Biblical times, and an ounce of gold could buy a fine men's suit today. That's a better return than holding paper money, which has an unfortunate history of always going to zero. Again, that's good news if there's inflation. But it doesn't trounce inflation the way investing in common stocks does. The stock market's average return of 7–8 percent on average over time is adjusted for inflation. That means we're talking about real returns adjusted for the decline of paper currency.

I tend to gravitate toward keeping 5 percent of my net worth in physical gold and silver and, when prices are in an upswing for the metals, another 5 percent in mining stocks and the like.

The biggest argument against owning precious metals is an important one. In short, physical metals just sit there and don't generate any cash flow in the form of interest or dividends. So by hunting through coin rolls to find silver as a child, I missed the opportunity to buy stocks that could have made me wealthier and paid dividends instead.

But here's the thing about missed opportunities: I also missed the opportunity to buy tech stocks in the late 1990s or housing stocks in the mid-2000s. Some opportunities prove to be worth missing out on over time. Although it's something all investors go through, it's just not worth second-guessing yourself all the time. Also, I was just starting my investment journey. If I had known everything I know today about investing and all the potential opportunities available, the decision to invest in silver still was one of the better ideas I could have carried out with the very limited capital of a child. I managed to identify an opportunity to make about five times my money with little to no risk, although it required a fair amount of labor.

While it's true that there's no cash flow in precious metals, at today's interest rate levels there's barely any income or cash flow out of bonds. I'd rather have some physical and tangible wealth than a piece of paper that can't keep up with inflation. That's why silver is one of the best trades I've ever made, and one that I likely won't ever completely cash out of. It could be the same for you too.

Using our three investment criteria, here's how I view this life-long and life-changing trade:

Safe: This trade seemed entirely safe at the time and, looking back on it, seems like one of the safest trades that anyone could have made. After all, I was acquiring silver coins at the face value of the coin, not at the silver content of the coin. Since silver has traded anywhere from $4–48 per ounce over the years I've owned it, these coins have traded anywhere from 4 to a whopping 192 times their face value.

Even if silver were to fall to zero, something that's never happened to any commodity before in human history, I would still have the face value of the coins and thus no real loss! That's the ultimate safe trade as far as I'm concerned.

I've also since learned that I'm not alone in making these trades. Online communities today still discuss the opportunities in what they call "coin roll hunting." While I'm sure you can still go to a bank and find some silver coinage, the potential finds aren't as good as they were 10, 20, or 30 years ago, given how things have been picked through. It's still a safe opportunity to increase your wealth. At $15 per ounce, a silver quarter is worth around $3.50, or 14 times its face value. But again, it's an investment that requires a substantial amount of time that, for most adults, just isn't worth it.

Debt-Free: I'll be honest; staying financially safe is a little bit of a problem with this trade, at least relative to other investments. With a stock, or even a silver ETF or the like, I can easily and quickly place in a sell order while the market is open. With physical precious metals, however, it's a different story.

I could go and sell my silver holdings to a coin or pawn shop at any time. While I'd get the best prices at a coin shop, it would still be a little bit below the spot price of silver—that's how coin shops stay in business. So owning physical metals has a lag to it that can weigh on our financial safety if we need to cash out in a hurry.

In the worst case scenario, where silver were to drop to zero, I could take the coins to a bank and exchange it for paper. I couldn't do that with, say, silver bars or other forms of silver that aren't recognized as money, however.

When silver does have a huge price spike, like it did in 2011 when it peaked at $48, silver coins will likely fetch a price close to spot. At those prices, people will be looking to cash out their old silverware, and other bric-a-brac that contains silver as well. Those forms of silver need to be weighed, their total silver content determined, and melted down and the like. That's not the case with 90 percent silver coinage. So in a panic buying period for silver, coins likely offer the best way to quickly cash out relative to other forms of the metal out there.

In short, the solvency isn't that much of a problem, but it is a little more difficult to go from physical silver to cash compared to trading stocks.

Rich: This "trade" essentially started my investment journey. It created a base of physical, tangible wealth to enjoy amid later investments in faster-moving investments like stocks or options. Because I was able to buy something at face value that was worth far more—and today is worth even more than that—it's a trade that, at times, has represented my best investment returns in a single trade.

It also goes to show the power of putting labor into an idea. I'll readily admit that I'm the least entrepreneurial member of my family. My parents and sister have all started and sold businesses. My only real business was in trying to earn a few extra bucks as a kid by washing cars and going through the neighbor's old coins for silver content.

Being willing to put effort, not just money, into an investment idea can substantially improve your returns. That's what I've found from my time spent scrounging for silver coins. If you're just looking to make money without that kind of work, as I've moved toward over the years, then investing in stocks is one of the best opportunities in town.

But just in case the stock market gets into trouble or there's huge political uncertainty, there's still value to be had owning precious metals like silver and gold. While we like to think that bad things can't happen in the United States, even "civilized" nations in Europe have had to deal with hyperinflation and massive government confiscations over the past 100 years.[1] Having tangible wealth that can be quickly moved isn't just valuable to avoiding a total loss of your wealth—it's invaluable.

CHAPTER 8

Catch the Boom, but Quit while You're Ahead

WHEN INVESTING IN MOST STOCKS—BUT especially commodity-based ones—knowing when to exit the trade is probably more important than knowing when to buy and enter the trade. A few key factors come to mind:

First, as with buying any investment, your timing will never be perfect. You'll never get out exactly at the peak. That's OK, as long as you're getting out close to the peak. If you're getting out of a trade with a huge, triple-digit percentage gain that's about to decline 40 percent, getting out within 5–10 percent of the peak price is still pretty precise for an investor.

Again, it's the same thing when buying an investment too. I'll often buy out-of-favor stocks that are within a few weeks or months of declining before they turn around—or have already started rallying after reaching a cycle low. If you try to wait for the exact bottom to buy, you'll likely never pull the trigger. It's not like there's a sign that pops up on your brokerage account telling you that *this* price is the bottom.

Second, when it comes time to selling a company, you'll want to look at simple valuation metrics to get an idea as to how your trade is doing compared to the overall market. If you bought shares in a company that are up 60 percent in the past year but the overall market is only up 10 percent, it's a good idea to see how the company is doing operationally.

If earnings and sales are still growing, then chances are there's still more room to run. If the share price is going up but the company's operations aren't improving, it may be sign that too many traders like shares here. That means there's plenty of demand for shares, so why not sell yours?

Then there's what I call "fuzzy accounting." Under US law, companies report their numbers quarterly. But behind those final earnings numbers are a number of accounting practices such as inventory write-downs, goodwill, and loss reserves that allow a company broad latitude between their revenue and their final earnings numbers.

Accounting issues can get pretty complex very quickly, so just bear in mind that it's not necessarily a red flag for investors. It is, however, certainly a yellow one that should be examined more closely. If a company starts having "one-time" accounting items every quarter, it might be better to sell and move on to an investment with a more understandable earnings report.

Finally, technological innovation can be a sign of an impending reason to sell a position. That's a tough one to gauge, because it can either help or hurt. The technological innovation of the Internet helped most companies rapidly expand their efficiency with the use of personal computers and global interconnectivity, but investing in some of the hot names of the dot-com bubble proved to be a disaster.

In the commodity space, technological change drove a bubble in the natural gas space in the mid-2000s. It made for a fantastic time to buy shares of exploration companies because of a promising new technology called fracking that would substantially increase natural gas production. It led to a boom, and as all commodity cycles work, it sowed the seeds for the eventual bust as well.

Let's take a look at how this played out:

On July 1, 2003, I purchased shares of a natural gas exploration company. I paid $9.57 per share. As I write today, those shares trade for $7.23—about a 25 percent loss nearly 14 years later.

But I'm not sitting on a loss. I booked a triple-digit gain, then got out of dodge. When shares rallied even after I sold, I'll admit I felt like I had cheated myself by getting out too early. But whenever I get that feeling about *any* trade I've made, I'll pull up this company and look at the chart going back to 2003.

The company is **Chesapeake Energy (CHK)**. And it might as well be two entirely different companies. The company that I was bullish enough to buy shares of back in 2003 was a sleepy little firm starting to make a big splash in the natural gas space. They were buying up areas with large pockets of the stuff, in shale formations everywhere from Texas to Pennsylvania. Their plan was to develop wells that would utilize a new technology known as fracking.[1]

Fracking is a way to extract smaller pockets of natural gas from areas previously thought depleted. It brought new life to seemingly dead assets. Wall Street loved the idea. After all, the United States is the Saudi Arabia of natural gas, and it had strong demand for energy. This technology would make it more readily available for use. The traders on Wall Street started cheering the company's every move to buy up more properties with gas-producing potential, even though the company was taking on higher levels of debt to do so.

The price rose faster than the company's valuation. I sold in August 2005 at $27.15. I had made 183 percent in just over two years. But more important, I had better investment opportunities elsewhere that I liked.

Shares traded higher, trading in early 2008 as high as $62. While I periodically checked the price and kicked myself mentally a bit for not being greedy enough, by the end of 2008 shares had been crushed down to $15—a loss of nearly 75 percent!

Following the financial crisis, shares of Chesapeake Energy traded between $15 and $30 for a few years, but began a major slide in mid-2014 that sent them even lower than what I paid for them back in 2003. At their low point in 2016, shares traded for under $3. That's 80 percent below their 2008 low.

What happened? The commodity boom went through a bust cycle. The success of fracking technology turned out to be bad for the industry, since it boosted production so much that natural gas prices dropped further than expected. The high debt taken on by the company in the boom years wasn't sustainable when cash flows from natural gas production, at lower prices, didn't work out.

Rather than add assets, lately, the company is looking to sell assets. And the company's founder and CEO was using his position to personally profit from a side business in some of the best cherry-picked fracking locations.[2] The board of directors convinced him to resign—but the company's reputation was subsequently so damaged that a major turnaround from that point will likely only come from higher natural gas prices, not from Chesapeake itself.[3]

So in hindsight, it's clear that knowing when to sell, even if it seems early, can spare a lot of pain. Someone paid $62 for shares that I sold at $27. They were too optimistic. By selling at $27 over a decade ago, I'm not holding shares at $7 today. I've managed to use the profits successfully in other trades as a result. That's the power of locking in an uncertain profit.

Let's run this older trade of mine—and its subsequent move—through our three investment factors and see how things worked out:

Safe: When I bought shares, I considered it more of a speculative play. After all, this was a bet on a commodity—and specifically, on a commodity with a promising technology behind it. It wasn't a well-established company with a consistent price for its goods that it could gradually raise over time. It was a company that had to sell its product at a wildly fluctuating market price—once they finally got around to production.

But even within the commodity space, some companies are safer than others. What made Chesapeake look safe as a bet compared to other natural gas explorers was its relative size compared to peers and how easy it was for the company to acquire debt to finance the properties it was purchasing. Buying a company on its way up, even if it isn't consistently making money yet, can usually mean catching a powerful trend that beats the market in the short term.

While Chesapeake Energy paid a modest dividend, which gave some safety in the form of returned cash, the company was also buying up new properties like gangbusters and taking on massive amounts of debt to do so. That meant that things would have to unfold exactly as optimistically as everyone was expecting for the trade to go well; otherwise, there could be problems down the line.

While I thought the company would do well, I didn't think it would do as well as it did. I was happy to more than double my money within such a short span of time. And while holding on longer might have meant even better returns, I can really only say that with the benefit of hindsight.

Debt-Free: This was an earlier trade of mine, when I was far younger and far less wealthy than I am today. I put my solvency at risk by putting a large percentage of my net worth into this position. Given the likelihood of solid, market-beating returns, however, it seemed like a risk worth taking. But I didn't buy options or do anything crazy where I could have been on the hook for *more* than I put into the trade. I put a lot of my cash at work, but it was my cash.

With most of my trades, my goal is to own shares for at least a year to get a favorable tax rate for long-term capital gains. I also want to get paid to wait for my investments to work out, so I'll always try to find a dividend-paying stock along the way. Chesapeake Energy offered both those prospects. Financial security is a lot easier to acquire with a long-term outlook than it is when you're trying to make a series of short-term trades.

Fortunately, as a company attracting strong speculative interest, there was ample trading volume in shares, so my stake could be easily absorbed by the market in the course of an average day's trading. That provided the solvency of liquidity, although that did periodically dry up during the share price declines in 2008 and 2014–16. But I wasn't invested in shares at that time.

Staying solvent and avoiding getting into financial challenges that could lead to debt will often mean taking profits on a winning stock. It will sometimes mean saving profits on a stock that is starting to act like a losing one. And whether you're successful or not depends on your time frame. I felt like an idiot for selling out of this company in early 2008, but by 2016, it's clear that a buy-and-hold strategy with a commodity-based company is a recipe for disaster.

Don't be afraid to take profits at a point you're comfortable with. Most money in investing has probably been lost by people trying to get an additional 5 or 10 percent out of a trade instead of simply cashing out with a profit that's "good enough."

Rich: This trade acted as a classic "take the money and run" situation, which periodically comes up in the commodity markets. I got in near a bottom and rode things part of the way up. I didn't get off at the top floor, but I didn't plummet back to the earth either.

The real secret to getting rich on this trade was being what I call "long-term greedy." That's where I'm not trying to maximize my returns on every single trade. Getting the exact highs and lows is impossible. Rather, what I'm looking to do is get in, make some money, and get out with a market-beating return before moving on to the next trade elsewhere.

Part of this trade also played to the market psychology at the time. In 2003, investors were still concerned about the risks of investing in technology stocks, but they still liked the idea of a new technology that could revolutionize other industries.

Fracking technology provided a bullish excuse for traders to buy into the natural gas story. But if fracking was going to be as successful as it seemed, it would create a boom in production that would lead to lower natural gas prices. That's exactly how it panned out. So this trade was more critical than others in terms of an exit strategy—if things worked as expected, the outcome would end up being bad for shares.

CHAPTER 9

Coal

When Everyone's Saying an Industry
Is Dead, It's Time to Buy

INVESTING IN COMMODITIES IS GREAT—DURING a bull market. It's not just that they go in the direction you want them to go; they tend to do so quickly. Far more quickly than stocks.

In the early 2000s, I was able to jump from one rally-ing commodity to the next. It was part of a global boom that eventually became part of the housing bubble that burst. In the post-financial crisis era, investing in commodities has become far more mixed as genuine economic growth has become more difficult. While many commodities rallied from their lows, low price inflation and weak demand meant that many commodities haven't hit new highs since.

What's more, many commodities reflated quickly after the crisis, only to falter when economic growth or inflation failed to materialize. The poster child for this phenomenon is gold, which went from $900 in 2009 to $1,900 in mid-2011 before starting to dive. The metal declined in price for five years before a mild rally in 2016.

Of course, gold is unique. It doesn't get used up or destroyed like other commodities. Rather, it gets hoarded, stored, saved, made into jewelry, and so on. It sticks around. Commodities that get used up rather than continually stockpiled had been beaten down just as bad and also looked interesting as a result.

In mid-2016, this brought me, and readers of my monthly investment newsletter *Crisis Point Investor*, to the coal sector. The United States has been compared to Saudi Arabia when it comes to our coal reserves.[1] We're swimming in the stuff. But unlike the Saudis, we aren't producing anywhere near our maximum output.

The problem is political. Since day one in office, President Obama has opposed the use of coal, and his EPA has been packed with anticoal officials.

It's easy to see why. After all, coal is a dirty burning fuel. Even with the use of CO_2 scrubbers and other technology to capture particulates, it's still not as clean as natural gas or nuclear power. That may not be a problem for a country like China or India with fast-growing energy needs. But for developed, wealthy nations like the United States that place at least some value on a clean environment, it is.[2]

It's no wonder that many coal companies are a shadow of their former selves. Arch Coal (ACI) filed for bankruptcy in January 2016. It was one of the larger players in the industry. What few well-paying blue-collar jobs in poverty-stricken Appalachia existed because of Arch Coal are now a memory.

Meanwhile, while this was going on in early 2016, another phenomenon was at work. Enter Donald Trump, who trounced his political opponents in the West Virginia primary on the promise to put America's coal miners back to work. According to the insurgent Trump campaign, it's time to make America great again, and nothing is as American as coal mining.[3] From anyone else running for president, that sentiment would sound like a political promise without the possibility of coming true. From Trump, it comes off as a clear conviction.

After all, it creates middle-class jobs for hardworking folks. And the coal doesn't have to be used domestically. We might as well take advantage of strong overseas demand for the stuff and export it abroad. That will benefit companies that have to transport the coal to its final destination as well.

While this might have sounded like the start of a turnaround for the coal industry at a time when the entire space appeared to be on its deathbed, it might have simply been another bump on the road. What's more, this wasn't the first time that coal prices (and coal companies) moved higher as a result of political posturing.

Back during the 2012 election, when polls put pro-coal candidate Mitt Romney near incumbent anticoal President Barack Obama, the beaten-down coal sector started rallying on expectations of a change in management. The rally wasn't much, and it started right before the election. It ended with the election as well. But since then, shares have continued on a downtrend culminating with high-profile bankruptcies at the start of 2016.

To me, a major company in the commodity space going bankrupt is a good sign that it might be time to start buying. It doesn't mean to necessarily make a huge bet, but it generally means that without one of the major players, the rest of the industry will now be closer to an equilibrium. Without the supply provided by the now-bankrupt company (or companies), and assuming demand doesn't drop off, prices are now in a position where they can stop falling. That's a good sign.

With the political and fundamental picture for coal looking better than expected, I advised readers of *Crisis Point Investor* to bet on the sector rather than individual stocks, as the best play going forward from mid-2016. Specifically, I advised the purchase of the **VanEck Vectors Coal ETF** (KOL).

From its inception in early 2008, this fund quickly soared from an initial price of $40 to $58. But since that peak, the stock began a long slide to around $8 in mid-2016, a whopping 86 percent loss, making it a dirt cheap bargain.

KOL wasn't just a play on the pro-America political outlook of Donald Trump. The ETF holds some global players, like China Shenhua Energy. And it also holds areas related to mining production like Joy Global. So it's not a pure play on the price of coal itself. When there's a gold rush, there's also a shovel rush and a jeans rush too. Likewise, when coal turns around, this ETF will turn around too. And in mid-2016, it seemed that coal's outlook couldn't get any worse. Typically, when things can't get any worse, they tend to get better. As I reminded readers in June 2016, coal is a commodity. Commodities always have some use. They never go to zero.

Yet for political reasons, commodities like coal have been heavily out of favor and in a downtrend for nearly eight years. Most commodities that drop 70 percent or more tend to stage strong counterrallies, *whether they end up getting back to their old highs or not*. With many traders likely burned by the investment at this point and unlikely to invest there again, interest was at an all-time low. That suggested that we could see a powerful counterrally soon, as investors least expected it.

In fact, looking over the ETF's chart, it had already once made a strong counterrally despite a long-term trend of overall declining prices. In late 2008, shares fell to $15 before surging back to $40 by 2011, as seen on the chart.

So what happened to our trade in 2016? Pretty much the same thing. Coal surged, and rather quickly too. In fact, we didn't even wait for the election part of the thesis to play out. I advised readers in *Crisis Point Investor* to take their profits on shares in our October issue, which released on September 26, 2016.

In just under four months, we made a return of 34.15 percent in this ETF, about what you'd expect to make on average in the stock market in about four years.

Shares continued to trend higher even after we sold—but with the election too close to call in late September, that paper gain could have become a very real loss. While Donald Trump was pro-coal, Hillary Clinton had come out strongly against the energy source, vowing to go even further than Barack Obama to end the industry.[4] With the possibility of another 2012 election result sending coal prices back down, it made more sense to lock in this large profit.

Let's see how this trade breaks down going through our three filters:

Safe: At first glance, trading in the coal mining space didn't look very safe. Coal as a commodity and coal stocks as companies have looked like terrible places to invest since 2012, if not earlier. Yet that glance at the price didn't tell us the facts about investing in the commodity space. If you knew that commodities have tremendous rallies followed by pullbacks that are just as big—if not bigger—then you'd realize that there was probably more upside than downside from here.

What's more, we were buying a diversified ETF that played coal from all angles: global, equipment and services providers, and the miners themselves. While a rising tide lifts all boats, and coal prices ended up rising, falling coal prices might not have fully reflected in the ETF thanks to some of these other positions.

Finally, coal prices seemed to be determined in substantial part by political considerations. As a result, prices had been in a downtrend in part due to actual political decisions by the EPA and other actors to keep a lid on coal in favor of more clean-burning fuels. So with this action already accounted for, any perception of a change in that direction made it likely that coal prices could recover. When viewed through that lens, the trade looked somewhat safer than expected.

Debt-Free: With only one trade to work with, a sector-wide ETF, we didn't have to make multiple buys across multiple companies. We could essentially concentrate on the idea as a whole. That helped us make a trade that fit this idea without spreading ourselves too thin—or owning companies that fell when the rest of the market rose, resulting in what's known as "diworseification."

We stayed financially safe by getting out of the trade before the election. Trump's opponent, Hillary Clinton, promised to continue pursuing policies that would make coal mining history. So coal's rally, a 34 percent return for me and my readers, wasn't as good as if I'd been able to time the absolute bottom the ETF hit in February 2016. From there, it closed the year about 140 percent higher.

So while the trade was great, it wasn't the kind of triple-digit slam-dunk that you could get investing in commodities without getting the timing exactly right 10–15 years ago. Sometimes there's a price to pay for solvency, but it's better to take a sizeable profit before a political event can undo it in the blink of an eye than try to hold on and risk losing it all.

Rich: Buying (or selling) commodities while they're on an uptrend (or downtrend) is a clear path to riches in just about any environment, so long as you don't overstay your welcome. This wasn't a clear path but rather what seemed to be a shift from one direction to another. The investment world is much more complicated when you have to consider the effects of political decisions and cheap money floating through the global financial system on top of the fundamental supply and demand for a commodity like coal.

However, with coal so beaten down already, it's clear that not only had many traders and investors lost money; they'd thrown in the towel. And with big companies in the sector like Arch Coal throwing in the towel, expectations were high that the down-trend would continue. But since commodities don't go to zero like stocks do, the secret to getting rich on this trade was to make a bet on the price of coal rising.

By mid-2016, the sector looked like it was on the brink of a terminal collapse. However, if there was even the possibility of coal continuing as a sector of the economy, sentiment would turn around. That's the difference between avoiding a potentially dangerous investment and taking a calculated risk. This trade worked—and quickly—because the bad news was all out and all priced in with nowhere else to go.

CHAPTER 10

Shipping

Always Make Money No Matter What Markets Are Doing

BY 2006, I WAS FEELING a little wary about investing in the commodity space. I had made money in copper, natural gas, timber, and the precious metals. Those investments had all seemed like fantastic bargains at the time, and my returns had certainly shown that to be the case as well.

But there didn't seem to be a new bargain among those areas. That's too bad, since a rallying commodity stock can make huge returns in a short space of time. Of course, when commodity prices are falling, those companies are the last place you want to be. But what happens when the space is no longer a bargain but it also doesn't look like it's going to fall anytime soon?

While many investors just focus on one area, like commodities, I prefer a jack-of-all-trades approach. It provides a lot more flexibility. As the old Wall Street saying goes, "There's always a bull market somewhere."

That got me thinking about another saying: "picks and shovels." Specifically, I was thinking about the California Gold Rush. The forty-niners who went out west to find a mother lode often ended up being disappointed. But merchants who went out west to supply the miners thrived as the population boomed.

In other words, sometimes as an investor, you need to look beyond where you're currently investing and think about the ancillary companies: those that provide services and goods to the companies that you are interested in. Doing so can allow you to find bigger and better bargains.

In my case, by 2006, I'd come to the conclusion that the best place to put my profits from investing in commodity stock was to buy a company in the shipping sector.

Again, it was a pretty simple decision once you got down to it. Demand for steel, iron, copper, and oil (among other commodities) was strong and rising. That's why those shares were doing well. But once those commodities were dug out of the ground, they needed to get to where they'd be used.

The shipping companies made sense as a result. Thanks to the increased demand for commodities, shipping rates had been heading higher, and most companies had already booked out their fleets. In fact, the industry was caught unprepared for the demand in global shipping, and there was a serious drought of ships. While many firms were contracting out to build new ships, it appeared that the world's needs wouldn't be fully met on that front for another two years. After all, this isn't World War II's command economy, which could build a Liberty ship in a day. Today's ships, specifically designed for the transport of cargo, can take upwards of a year to build.[1]

Shipping stocks were already starting to form an uptrend, something that I like to see when buying for the first time. After looking over the industry as a whole, I decided to put my money on Diana Shipping (DSX). Besides being in the right sector, the company had a great valuation. It had little debt, a fully booked fleet, and paid a sizeable dividend as well. Since it could take a few years for new ships to round out the global shipping fleet and meet demand, there was a tremendous appeal in getting paid to wait.

In early 2006 when I bought, shares of Diana Shipping traded around $10 per share. That was a reasonable price, coupled with its low debt and price-to-earnings ratio that made it a bargain on a conventional basis as well.

What I didn't expect was how quickly rotating to this value in the market would pay off. By the end of the year, shares were up to $15. Within a year they were up to $20. Finally, between July and September of 2007, shares rose from $26 to $42. Sometimes a trade goes the way you expect—and sometimes a trade ends up going even better than you could possibly expect!

I had sold out half my stake around $20, which meant I still owned shares but had gotten my original stake back. I finally sold the second half around $30 shortly later, when it looked like shares had simply run up too far, too fast. While I was surprised to see how far shares continued to rise after I had sold, I didn't get emotional and kick myself for the potential gains I could have had if I had patience.

Why? Because the situation was different. The story on the global shippers was out, as shipping rates continued to rise. The new ships being built were finally hitting the global shipping lanes, and it was likely that shipping rates would start falling. As that happened, the current levels of cash flow and profitability for the shipping companies would peak and decline—sending shares right back down again.

While I prefer giving trades a few years to play out, the existing value that was in Diana Shipping shares a year ago just wasn't there. It was time to cash out so that I could put money to work in the next value as it appeared.

Indeed, that proved to be the case. The shipping stocks were in the midst of a false prosperity, as mid-2007 marked the peak for most stocks, commodities, and other investments ahead of the financial crisis.

In fact, if you fast forward to today, Diana Shipping looks like an entirely different company. As new ships were built and added to the global shipping fleet, the drought of shipping space became a glut as global trade was brought to a standstill. As global shipping rates plummeted, Diana's cash flow started to decline. The dividend was eliminated, and the company took on sizeable debt.

Amazingly, Diana is still one of the better companies in the shipping space. Other firms have more debt or have been worse from an operational standpoint in the post–financial crisis world of slow global trade.

Today, shares now trade at less than $4. In other words, if you bought and held shares in 2006, you would have lost 60 percent of your money in 10 years. Because of the company's deteriorating financial situation, however, most investors looking solely at those results would have likely gotten out of the trade long before that sizeable loss.

That underscores how critical it is for investors to monitor their positions regularly and make changes as needed to preserve and grow their wealth. Suffice to say, unless things look to turn around again or the shipping companies vastly improve their cash flow, it's a sector worth avoiding for the foreseeable future.

Here's how the trade looks through the lens of our three criteria:

Safe: This trade fit the criteria for being safe on both sides of the trade. When looking to buy, I was looking for a sector of the economy that could benefit from the global commodity boom but hadn't made as big a move as the commodity stocks. I found that with the shipping sector. It was a classic "pick and shovel" play also. Specific to Diana was a great balance sheet and a high dividend payout as well. This was a company that clearly looked like it was being managed for the benefit of shareholders, and so I'd be paid to wait for the thesis to play out.

Because the trade became a double quickly, there was also safety in being able to exit the trade as well. As a general rule, I'll sell any position that's doubled within the space of a year. That means I've taken nearly all the risk off the table, and if the stock goes higher, great. If it starts to decline or the fundamentals of the company change, I can sell out there too, but there's no fear of a real loss anymore once the original capital is out of the trade.

Debt-Free: This trade was initially purchased out of profits from prior trades. So there was little risk going in that the money would need to be available at an inopportune moment. What's more, given the decision to sell half the stake after it had doubled meant an increase in cash. Finally, when shares started rising at an unsustainable rate, I didn't wait for the stock to top out and crash. I took profits, even though over the short term it looked like a mistake.

On a broader scale, getting out of rapidly rising trades like this one in mid-2007 meant a lot of capital to put to work. But the bargains that had existed just a year ago were nowhere to be found. As a result, I ended 2007 with a large cash stake. Within a year, that would start to be put to use as the financial crisis unfolded and a universe of bargain stocks emerged. The overall discipline in this trade illustrates the importance of being willing to take profits before getting too greedy and having the patience to wait for a clearly good trade to emerge.

Rich: Identifying any trade that can double within the space of a year requires a willingness to see where the market is undervalued and where things are likely to head. It also takes the good fortune that others in the market will see the same thing you do, at least *after* you buy.

Preserving that gain is also important as well. As we've seen with this example, taking profits off the table on a position that's quickly rallied doesn't just keep you financially secure. It keeps you from possibly losing money on the trade no matter what happens in the future.

Just remember, no company has a strategic advantage forever. That's especially true in the commodity space, and companies that service the commodity sector. It's impossible to go broke if you keep taking profits, even if the stock trades higher after you sell. So what? If you're trying to grow and keep your wealth, taking profits is the name of the game.

CHAPTER 11

Gold

Betting on a Counterrally in Oversold Commodities

I LOVE THE COMMODITY SPACE for its big moves. Of course, that's provided that I'm on the right side of such a move. When commodity prices change, they can be far more volatile than other stocks. That means a higher likelihood of getting a bigger percentage return. If you're making the right trade, a few small investments in the commodity space can perform far better than core holdings like dividend-paying stocks in other sectors.

And while commodities are volatile, they don't go to zero. There's no world where oil or gold or corn would be worth nothing. Even if society finds fewer uses for something, there's still a residual value. For instance, while we use cars for transportation today, we still value horses, even though we don't use them to travel anymore. In fact, owning a horse has gone from being a necessity for most folks to a luxury. Many breeds can fetch fantastic prices for those interested in owning a prized horse.

The point I'm trying to make is that when things look so out of favor for a commodity that it seems like it *could* go to zero, you'll probably want to make a big fat trade going on the long side.

For instance, gold entered into a bull market around 2003, gradually rising from around $300 an ounce to nearly $1,000 by 2008. And after getting knocked down by the financial crisis a bit, gold prices came back with a vengeance, surging to nearly $1,900 per ounce just three years later, in 2011.

But prices rose so far, so fast that the market turned sour. Gold demand dropped amid the high prices. Gold ended up making a five-year bear market after its eight-year bull market before turning up again in 2016.

If you had bought gold in 2011, you were out of luck. But if you had bought the metal in 2003, you were still doing pretty well. What's more, you had an asset that outperformed the stock market much of the time.

But when gold started dropping under $1,100 in early 2016, it had sold off too far, too fast. Gold seemed ripe for a bounce. Whether that would be the start of a new bull market for the metal or simply a counterrally amid the bear market remained to be seen. But the opportunity was there. Gold demand was rising, and years of falling prices were finally leading to a drop in supply. Even better, the gold mining companies were finding ways to slash costs, meaning their profitability could substantially improve even if gold prices didn't move at all.

With all of these factors at stake, I advised members of the *Braintrust* investment service to make a bet on gold on the long side. I expected the metal had been oversold and would soon shoot up 5–10 percent.

While that wasn't a phenomenally huge move, for a market the size of gold, it's still a sizeable change. But we could do better than just buy the metal or an ETF that tracked the price of gold.

In the commodity space, you get bigger percentage moves out of companies that provide those commodities than you do out of the underlying item itself. If copper goes up 10 percent in price, a company that produces copper might go up 20 or 30 percent. That makes commodity-producing stocks the best place to invest your money in a bull market for those items. Conversely, it's the last place to keep your money when the commodity starts going down.

But when you have a situation like with gold in early 2016, where the trend *might* be reversing but might *also* be a rally within the broader context of a bear market, you don't need to buy and hold forever. Rather, the optimal approach is to simply buy something as leveraged as possible, look for a quick gain, and then get out.

That's what I did with gold in 2016 for myself and my *Braintrust* subscribers. We bought January 2017 $30 call options on the **Van Eck Gold Miners ETF (GDX)**. Rather than bet on one gold company, we would be betting on a basket of the major gold miners to make a big move should gold rise 5–10 percent as expected. We used the call option because it would benefit the most, in percentage terms, from rising gold prices.

We bought these options on April 13 at $1.19 per contract. At the time, GDX traded around $22.25 per share. In order for these options to go in-the-money, the ETF would have to rally by 33 percent. That sounds steep but also in line with a large move in gold.

More important, these options would increase in value as shares went higher. If prices rose quickly enough, there would be no need to wait for the trade to close in on its expiration date. Instead, we could simply take profits whenever we wanted.

As it turned out, our timing was excellent. We closed out the trade on June 15, 2016. GDX was closing in on the $30 price range within two months of the trade. We sold the option at $2.49 per contract, a gain of 109.2 percent.

Why sell after two months when there was still six months left on the option? For starters, the situation in gold had done a complete 180 turnaround in the two months we were in the trade. The metal had reversed its losses and posted strong gains. Gold stocks were rallying like gangbusters—but had gone up too far, too quickly. When any asset makes big gains like the gold stocks were making in a short period of time, it's better to take profits and wait for a more sustainable trend to emerge.

Second, despite the strong rally in gold, there was no indication that this was the start of a bigger move. Rather, it appeared that gold's early 2016 losses were simply unwinding, and investors were getting more interested in gold but not enough to spark a renewed bull market after being out of favor for half a decade.

That was the rationale at the time. We had more than doubled our money and turned every $119 into $249. But if the GDX had stalled there, that option would have lost its entire time premium and gone to zero.

In fact, as I write at the end of 2016, the GDX now trades under $20, not under $30. Gold prices haven't held their big gains from the first half of 2016. But investors who bought GDX back in January are still up 50 percent just on that ETF. Had an investor just bought gold, they'd have underperformed stocks yet again . . . although they'd at least have a gain this year. The gold miners, on the other hand, have held up much better thanks to gold's downtrend at least ending this year.

But whether you're investing in gold, silver, copper, pork belly, or any other commodity, a few lessons here are clear. Buy shares of companies that produce those commodities, not the commodity itself. In an upswing, your profits will be bigger. Don't be afraid to buy options on those companies either, especially if you can get in relatively cheaply. And don't be too concerned about taking profits. In the commodity space, a big profit today can turn into a loss tomorrow—or more gradually as the case of this trade and subsequent performance shows.

Those are the lessons on investing in commodity price swings that I've learned over the years through trial and error. Even with this knowledge, sometimes a trade will go against you. Don't beat yourself up over the occasional loss. It's all part of the investment game.

Let's run this trade through our three filters to see how well it met our investment criteria:

Safe: I view this trade as speculative, but ultimately safe. It's safe because, by buying a call option, the most money I could lose would be the money I put into the trade. With each option originally selling at around $119 per contract, it would have been easy for any investor to buy the option and play the gold market without putting too much money at risk. You couldn't even buy 1/10 of an ounce of gold at that price!

Second, by buying an option with a January expiration date in April, there were eight months for the trade to play out. But I expected gold to rally within three to six months as sentiment in the commodity space improved. Having that extra time meant paying more of an option premium to enter the trade, but it also meant that there would be wiggle room for the trade if it didn't pan out as expected.

And the trade *didn't* pan out as expected—it only took two months for the trade to play out! We've also seen with the subsequent decline in gold prices that this trade's profits were taken at the perfect time as well. Holding on for the prospect of more gains would have meant lower returns at best or, at worst, a losing trade instead!

Debt-Free: This is a trade where solvency depended on two things. First, going into the trade, it was critical not to put too much capital into the position. Given the expected event of higher gold prices, buying the call option was the least expensive choice. It allowed for the biggest percentage move without having to buy shares outright of the Gold Miners ETF or any individual gold mining companies. And buying the option made it far easier to get in and out of the trade, and cost less in commissions, than buying gold at a coin or bullion shop!

The other aspect of solvency was being willing to exit the trade even though it seemed as though the gains would continue endlessly. With an options trade that had doubled within the space of two months, the gains were just too good to pass up. It's important to treat commodity trades a bit more as speculations. While you can let a winning telecom or insurance stock continue to ride in your portfolio, it's not the best idea with an options trade.

Putting up a small amount of cash up front and being willing to take profits quickly is always a winning combination for staying solvent, controlling a big stake without going into debt to do so, and keeping your portfolio growing at a market-beating rate.

Rich: It's pretty clear how the trade helped me add to my wealth. I bought something, it went up, I sold it. But more important, it was a prudent speculation where the timing proved to be fantastic. Even if you only use a small part of your portfolio for trades where you can quickly double or triple a small amount of money, it's tough to find more than a handful of such trades each year.

The critical notion about this example, however, is that these trades *can* be done more often than you think. If you expect an asset to do well, you don't need to buy that specific asset. In the case of many commodities, like, say, pork belly, you wouldn't want to take physical possession anyway. The lesson here is to find ways to leverage your expectations and, if possible, lessen the amount of risk and capital you put into the trade.

Many stocks have 5–10 percent moves in a given month, but the constant up-and-down motions of the stock market as a whole lead to gains of around 8 percent per year on average over time. Finding a stock that's beaten down and prime for a bump, even a small one, can become a far bigger return with the use of options instead. And since each option is for 100 shares of a company's stock but trades at a discounted cost compared to buying those shares, you can make more with less thanks to the use of options. You don't even need to be in the commodity space to use this strategy.

PART III

SHORT TRADES

Markets go up—and markets go down. While they mostly go up, when markets do decline, it's often steeper and quicker than the prior rally up. That's why it's important to consider both sides of the market.

In this part, we'll look at trades I've made on the short side of the market and what to look for when you're trying to profit from declining sectors, commodities, or even individual stocks. These trades shouldn't be a major part of your portfolio, nor do they even need to be part of your portfolio most of the time. But being able to navigate this half of the market is one of the more powerful ways to preserve your wealth during market fears.

CHAPTER 12

Beating the Bear

Making Profits as the S&P 500 Index Drops

IT'S TRUE THAT, OVER TIME, markets will trend up. Yet they also have periods where they go down. And when they do go down, they can unwind months or even years of gains in a very short amount of time.

I see market pullbacks as a feature, not a flaw. If stocks always went up, you'd have no incentive to do any real research. It would make more sense to put all your money into stocks now, and even borrow as much as possible to do so. But stocks come down for a variety of reasons. Usually, it's just because investors have gotten too optimistic too quickly and prices need to come back down for a bit as short-term profits are taken.

But as an individual stock or the market as a whole approaches a 10 percent decline from its recent peak, fear tends to set in. That gives us opportunities as investors. First, we can start buying shares at a sizeable discount compared to where they recently traded. Alternatively, we can also play on the fears by joining the market on the short side.

I don't like to directly "short stocks." That's a practice where you borrow shares you don't own and then sell them on the open market. You're hoping to buy back the shares later after the price has dropped. While that sounds neat in theory, in order to borrow shares, you have to pay anywhere from 5 to 50 percent per year. So if you're going to directly short stocks, you need the position to drop quickly before you bleed on the trade thanks to carrying costs.

What's more, if you short a dividend-paying stock, you also get to pay the dividend to the shareholder you borrowed from. That's another cost as well.

And even if everything goes your way, the most you can make on a trade is 100 percent—because that's how far a stock can fall percentage-wise from where you sold. However, if you short a stock at $10 and it jumps to $50, your losses can very quickly exceed 100 percent of your capital.

Fortunately, there's a better way to go short. It involves buying put options instead.

When you buy an option, the most you can lose is what you put into that trade. And an option provides leverage. That could turn a 10 percent market decline into a 100 percent win for you if you do it right. After the market has had a brief and powerful rally, or getting into certain months of the year, I've found it profitable more often than not to buy put options betting on a market decline.

On October 14, 2014, I put out just such a trade for investors of the *Insider Hotline* trading service that I run. Markets had been jittery for a few weeks, and corporate insiders weren't buying shares at these prices. I suspected that these folks—from CEOs to vice presidents and the like—were waiting for better prices after the market's solid rally so far that year.

That meant stocks were likely to fall a bit more, even though the S&P 500 Index was already closing in on a 10 percent correction from its recent highs.

I didn't see a need to close out any of the existing trades we had—they would mostly collect dividends in a market pullback and were fundamentally sound in terms of how the underlying companies were performing.

Because it was already mid-October, and stocks tend to start rallying around Thanksgiving and into the New Year—the so-called Santa Claus rally—I figured an options trade would be perfect here. It was the kind of position where we could make 15–25 percent or so over the next few weeks as stocks continued to trend lower.

With that in mind, I put out an alert to buy the January 2015 $150 put options, which were selling at $0.85. Since every option is for 100 shares, it was really $85 per contract. But at that price, investors could easily build up a hedge position designed to rise as the overall market fell. And since there's heavy volume on S&P 500 options, getting into and out of these trades is far easier than a lot of the other options trades that I like to make in individual stocks.

Again, this was a small trade designed to help make some money while the market was falling. I've found that many investors will be willing to throw in the towel on their investments at the worst time: during small, periodic—but temporary—market pullbacks like the one we faced in October 2014. Finding small trades like this that can profit when markets are weak provides a place to focus on the short term where it really matters, so that you can continue to stay invested for the long term without the powerful sense of dread that can sometimes kick in.

But we ended up closing the trade the next day. On October 15, markets had their worst day in weeks, dumping nearly 3 percent at their worst. But as stocks started to come off their lows during the middle of the trading day, it looked like the recent bear market was starting to break. Investors were starting to step in and buy shares as the markets closed in on a nearly exact 10 percent drop from their recent highs.

Our put option trade, less than a day old, had surged to $1.59, or $159 per contract. Again, that doesn't sound like much if you just made the one trade. But based on our entry price of $0.85, we managed to eke out a one-day gain of 87.06 percent.

The next few trading days confirmed my suspicions. Because the market started to turn around after its worst trading day yet, it was likely that the short-term bottom was in and stocks would now start to head up after a few weeks of scaring investors to the sidelines.

This is one of the more clear-cut examples of using put options to profit from a declining market. If your timing is perfect, you can make a tremendous amount of money on the short side to off-set the drop in price on your declining long positions. You don't need to go too wild, and can find options trades for less than $100 per contract that can help protect your money from the swipe of a bear market.

In the two years since that trade, I've yet to have a repeat of that perfect timing. But that's OK—as long as you're hedging when things look overextended or when fear is starting to creep into the market, you'll feel a lot better knowing that you have a trade out designed to benefit from falling prices. Just don't go too crazy—stocks tend to rise over time, so it's not a trade you'll want (or even need) to have open all the time.

Let's see how this trade fit into our three investment parameters:

Safe: When faced with a declining market, there are a lot of choices to make. Should you sell an existing position? Or more than one position? How much? And what happens after the sale if the market turns around? It seems that the safest course of action when markets are risky is to hedge first.

That's exactly what this kind of options trade is. It's something investors can do as markets start to get wild. That way, if things get better instead, you haven't made the mistake of selling out of a position at the worst time. Staying safe, first and foremost, means using the long-term investment power of the markets to your advantage. Brief sell-offs can create the illusion that it's time to head to cash when it really isn't.

By hedging, if stocks go down, part of your portfolio will continue to go down, but now a part of it will rise as well. That provides a margin of safety in the very short term for most small market sell-offs. Over time, however, given how markets tend to rise far more than they fall, you don't want to be permanently hedged, otherwise you won't make anywhere near as much money (if any at all). By using an options trade, you can get into and out of the short side of the market quickly as events warrant. You don't have to be stuck in a bad trade.

Finally, this trade allowed us to go short, but without putting up large sums of capital. That's the beauty of options trading. While the leverage can magnify both gains and losses, it can also reduce the amount of money you need to protect your portfolio from fluctuating markets.

Debt-Free: This trade, and many others like it that I've made, are designed with solvency in mind. Since we're not directly shorting stocks or the index but using options instead, our losses are capped by the amount we put into the trade. Anyone buying a single option would have risked $85, an amount of capital that can easily be recovered, even if this specific trade had been a complete loss.

Had I chosen to short the entire market instead, I might have done well for a day, but then faced margin calls and financial ruin as stocks ended up turning around. Even if my timing had been off on the options trade, I couldn't have lost a penny more than what I put into the trade.

This trade also shows that investors don't need to hedge our entire portfolio dollar for dollar either. We just need to have a big enough position to generate some extra money on one of the market's down days. It might not fully offset what we lose on the long side, but since markets tend to rise over time, our long positions take care of themselves in time as well.

In this case, we had options that nearly doubled as the market fell 3 percent in a day. While it's painful to see an entire portfolio shed that much in a day, it can and does happen. Knowing how to make a trade that can offset that kind of one-day decline helps ensure that you're staying solvent without having to panic out and go to cash.

Rich: With this trade, we expanded our investment universe. Rather than look at an opportunity to buy a stock, hold on to it, collect dividends, and hope that it rose in value, we were able to look at the market as a whole and profit from one of its numerous declines. Since the end of the financial crisis, these declines have been benign in nature. The market has fallen about 10 percent from its recent highs before buyers have come in to find some bargains and send stocks back up again.

Many individual stocks have fallen far more on a percentage basis in recent years however, and some of the best investment opportunities on the long side as the current bull market in stocks has stretched on have come from buying these specific names while they've been out of favor.

But those trades take time, and investors watching markets fall in the present might become fearful about their long positions. That's why options trades like these give us two ways to profit. First, there's the gain from making the actual put option trade—buying low and selling higher. Second, there's the future gain from holding on to existing long positions and ignoring them during the market's downturn.

I certainly prefer having trades like this to distract while the market is dropping, as it gives me better focus on what's going on—specifically *why* the market is falling. If I'm investing right on the long side, the only thing I need to think about during a market correction is which positions to add to and at what price. That's the secret to getting rich over time, and options trades like this can help put that into perspective.

CHAPTER 13

Using Options to Profit from Falling Commodity Prices

SHORTING, OR TRYING TO MAKE a profit when prices go down, isn't just relegated to an individual stock or the market as a whole. It can be used in just about any tradeable asset.

The commodity space is ripe for short-selling opportunities. While I love commodity investments when they're on a sharp uptrend because of their market-beating characteristics, the opposite is also true. When commodities fall out of favor, their prices drop phenomenally fast.

After all, commodities have no brand loyalty. A barrel of oil from one company is the same as a barrel from another. A copper bar from one company is the same as another. They trade at the same price because they're the same. There's no brand to hide behind or otherwise offset falling prices. When prices are high, supply explodes. High-cost producers can make money at high prices, and low-cost producers are making a huge profit margin as a result. When things decline, the high-cost producers go out of business, and the low-cost producers stay to survive into the next cycle, even if their profitability is hurt in the short term.

Even better, the commodity space is often dominated by a few names. The closure of a key copper mine in Peru may send prices soaring. The shutdown of a single oil refinery on the Gulf coast might send gas prices up in the United States.

The fewer the number of players, the more clout an individual player has to affect prices. For instance, China has played its hand well with its vast resources of REEs—rare-earth elements. Any news from China on these elements will instantly change global prices. Clearly, when there's only one player, it's a little harder to find an investment opportunity. You need a market with multiple key players, but not so many that it's overwhelming to keep track of.

Oil provides the best example of profiting from a drop in commodity prices in recent years. Since the end of the financial crisis, oil promptly rose from crisis-level prices of $30 per barrel to around $100. But it didn't trend much higher. Instead, oil prices spent several years trading in a range between $80 and $100 per barrel. This was a period of stability, with modest growth in global demand being met with new supplies or existing supplies supplemented with better technologies.

And then OPEC, the Organization of Petroleum Exporting Countries, threw the stability out the window.

To be fair, OPEC was concerned about the rising output of nonmember nations, particularly the United States. With oil prices trending between $80 and $100, it was economically feasible to extract formerly inaccessible sources of oil in shale formations—usually inaccessible rocky geologic formations.

While oil prices had already started their seasonal downtrend, on Thanksgiving Day 2014, OPEC met. While Americans were enjoying turkey and football, the cartel decided to bring oil prices down even further by increasing their production to its maximum capacity.

By expanding production, OPEC was hoping that lower prices would result. These lower prices would make oil production in shale formations (and in nonmember nations overall as well) too expensive to undertake. This would mean a decline in production outside of OPEC, and the oil cartel would, in turn, reverse the trend of its declining market share in recent years.[1]

But think about what OPEC was really saying: they were giving investors the green light to continue shorting oil and oil stocks beyond the seasonal decline that the market was already facing! In other words, the next few months would likely mean even lower oil prices as the supply on the market would now exceed the demand.

That meant good news and bad news. At the gas pump, it would mean good news as lower prices would likely endure for longer. As an investor, it would mean bad news. The energy sector is a large component of the overall stock market, and falling prices would impact earnings in that sector substantially.

But commodity prices are self-correcting. If prices get too low, shortages appear and prices go back up. So any decline in oil prices seemed likely to be a short-term phenomenon that would play out over a few months before prices found a new home at a price below the $80–100 range they had traded in for years before.

To profit from the adjustment to that new and lower trading range, the best opportunity seemed to be in shorting oil. As with other positions going short the market, buying put options seemed like the best risk-adjusted way to profit from oil's likely further decline.

On December 1, 2014, I put out a trade for *Insider Hotline* subscribers to buy the July 2015 US Oil Fund (USO) $20 put options. These options traded at $0.57, or just $57 per contract. At that price, it would be easy for investors to scale into the trade depending on how much they wanted to try to profit from oil's decline or how much they were looking to hedge their existing energy positions against a probable bear market for oil.

As expected, oil prices continued to decline. But the decline wasn't orderly. The OPEC meeting and decision to produce at maximum capacity led to a panic in the market. Oil prices were now sliding toward the $50 range after having traded at nearly double that at the start of the summer.

By December 12, it was time to take profits on the trade. Oil prices had gone down just about daily since the OPEC meeting, and nothing moves in a straight line forever. The options had also increased to $1.68, or $168 per contract. That meant that within the space of 11 days, we had made 194.73 percent betting against oil—after waiting for OPEC's green light for us to do so!

We don't get many opportunities to profit from big, fast swings. Typically, a commodity rally will take years, but the corresponding bear market that unwinds that rally can take weeks or months. Most commodities don't have a third-party like OPEC behind them to act like a wild card and swing markets either. Remember, oil prices had already started to slide. OPEC just gave an additional push that sent the oil markets out of their seasonal decline and into a full-blown panic.

Once again, let's run the trade through our three criteria and see how it did:

Safe: As with our other short trades, we weren't really short. Since directly shorting limits the potential profits but can also create a scenario where losses could be unlimited, we don't want to directly short a position. It doesn't matter if it's a stock or a commodity like oil. We want to short by buying put options. That limits our risk to the amount of capital we put into the trade. That way, had the trade gone against us, the most we would have lost would have been $57 per contract.

We kept this trade safe by using a widely traded oil ETF with a variety of high-volume options available to trade. And by using a far out-of-the-money strike price on the option, we were betting that oil prices would fall hard and deliver huge returns relative to a small amount of capital at risk.

Finally, even though this trade went from start to finish in less than two weeks, the option strike date was just over eight months out from the initial purchase date. That gave plenty of time for the trade to play out, just in case the trade did stall.

While the plan with buying put options is to close them out before they expire, sometimes Mr. Market goes your way in a matter of days or weeks, and sometimes things don't go your way (or go your way quickly and severely enough). It's good to give yourself as much time as possible, even on a trade you don't expect to hold for that long. Trades often can, and will, go against you before improving.

Debt-Free: We avoided financial danger with this trade in a few ways. First, as with staying safe, we didn't directly short oil. That means that we avoided unlimited losses had oil prices mysteriously started going ever upward (that's more likely to happen with a common stock than a commodity, but it's still the biggest risk with shorting). Our overall risk was limited, and each contract was for such a small sum of money, just about any investor could have gotten into the trade, no matter what the size of their portfolio was. That kept us out of debt.

What's more, we got out of the trade relatively quickly—we were invested for a mere 11 days, including nontrading weekends. We didn't try to wait for oil prices to hit their ultimate low. As of this writing, it seems that the low for this oil bear market was in February 2016, over a year after this trade had ended and more than six months after the options would have expired. Part of staying financially safe is to take big, quick profits off the table, even if there's a chance for bigger profits down the road. Basically, we stayed solvent on the trade by taking profits rather than getting too greedy.

By getting out of the trade quickly and locking in profits, we didn't run the risk of the trade going against us. Oil prices could have easily started to rally again following their steep and sudden loss. Or oil prices could have gone flat for a while, which would have also ruined the trade since options will lose a little bit of their time value every day. Trading with options is a bit like a game of hot potato: you may have more time left on the clock, but it's better to get out while you're substantially ahead of the trade.

Rich: I viewed this trade as an opportunity to get rich on a few fronts. First, there're the quick profits available from any fast trade that more than doubles your money in less than a month. These opportunities are few and far between. While the markets can move fast, they usually don't unless there's some kind of event like an earnings report for a company. In our case, we had a fast move because OPEC told us they were now willing to drive down prices if it meant they could improve their declining market share. That's a rationale for a trade that won't last forever, but will last long enough to provide some excellent investment opportunities.

Also, OPEC was telling us to bet against the energy sector in the short term. But that's a huge slice of the economy and stock market where investors often buy and hold over the long haul. Since many investors own energy stocks, even if it's just in a fund, falling oil prices mean that their portfolio values will take a short-term dive as the oil bear market gets under way. So to some extent, this trade also acted as a hedge against any existing portfolio positions that an investor might have held.

Third, because of OPEC's actions, this trade acted as a signal that the comfortable $80–100 range that oil prices had been in for some time was now over. A new trend would emerge, making some wealthier and some poorer. So while there was this short-term trade to profit from, I also took the opportunity to sell off some of my energy holdings at the same time before this new pattern emerged. Some of those sales were at a loss. While that was painful, the trade showed how quickly oil prices started to drop in 2014. Staying invested in those companies, even the supposedly "safe" major integrated oil names, would have led to even bigger losses.

In short, this trade acted a lot like an iceberg. On the surface were massive profits. But underneath, it also signaled a shift in the entire energy sector—a sign that it was time to significantly lighten up on long positions. Those kinds of signals are rare, but following them is critical to staying safe, debt-free, and rich when markets swing from bullish to bearish as oil did in late 2014.

CHAPTER 14

The Most Volatile—but Profitable—Trades I've Ever Made

THIS IS EITHER THE SMARTEST series of trades I've ever made . . . or the stupidest. I'm still not sure, even though it's consistently worked for me over the past six years. It's the final case study that I want to share with you regarding short trades. It's also the most complex, and there's a lot of explanation behind it.

This moneymaking trade isn't for everyone. It's wild, it's crazy, and it takes a lot of explanation. But I've found that it's been a great way to make extra returns. What is this trading strategy? Shorting market volatility.

What's volatility? Simple. It's essentially how much an asset moves over a given time period. If a stock moves an average of 1 percent a day—up or down—it's less volatile than a stock that moves an average of 5 percent a day. Since volatility is measured in percentage terms, it's easy to compare across different stocks, or even gauge the market itself.

Of course, volatility changes over time. During a market panic, stocks will move a lot more on average. During the financial crisis, the stock market posted some extreme moves both down *and* up.

Volatility is traditionally measured by the *Volatility Index*, or VIX. It's on a scale of 1 to 100, and at its core, it looks at the ratio of bullish options bets being made by traders compared to bearish options bets. So the VIX usually trades around an average of 17 to 20, reflecting the fact that markets tend to rise more often than they fall. During periods of calm, like during the past few years, the VIX has fallen as low as 11 to 12. During periods of panic, the VIX can quickly spike up. At the height of the financial crisis, the VIX hit 70.

That's volatility, both as a concept and as it's understood by Wall Street traders. While the index has been around since the early 1990s, it really only took off during the financial crisis.[1] Since then, it's attracted a lot of attention from traders.

That brings us to the next question: How do you trade volatility? With the explosion of exchange traded funds (ETFs) and exchange traded notes (ETNs), there are volatility-specific ways to play the market. The one I follow the most is the **iPath S&P 500 Volatility Index Short-Term Futures ETN (VXX)**.

But remember, volatility isn't tangible like a stock or bond. There's no "there" there. It's just a measure of how jumpy the market looks based on how the options market is trading. Essentially, that makes volatility trades a derivative of a derivative. It's so out of touch with the reality of investing that these products make very little sense. That is, unless you're willing to short volatility during some of the market's periodic crises.

This also ties in to the one big disadvantage of owning a fund: they all have a tracking error. A tracking error occurs when a fund doesn't perform in line with the underlying securities it holds. Any fund that charges a fee, will, over time, have results that deviate from whatever index it's tracking for performance.

Even a low-cost fund with a 0.10 percent annual fee will eventually create a sizeable tracking error.

Besides fees, errors can occur from significant buying and selling in a fund or ETF that causes it to move noticeably away from its *net asset value* (NAV). When too many buyers surge into an ETF, the fund might not be able to keep up with the deluge. Until they put that cash to work to buy more shares, every $1 that an ETF buyer puts in will only buy them less than $1 in value. That's not a winning proposition.

Finally, one of the biggest errors that funds have results from leverage. Double- and triple-leveraged products are the worst. Over time, they'll get extremely far away from the index they're supposed to track. Think about it this way: You have a fund with a value of $100. It falls 1 percent one day, then rises 1 percent the next day. How much do you have? Less than $100. On day one, the 1 percent decline from 100 results in a total value of $99. A 1 percent gain from $99 leads to a return by the end of day two at $99.99. These small errors magnify over time and with the use of leverage.

Again, this is a problem with all funds, even the most inexpensively managed index-tracking ones. But we're past traditional funds here—we're dealing with a highly leveraged derivative of a derivative. The tracking error on volatility products is huge. I've yet to find a worse place in terms of tracking error. This error means that even if volatility surges, the funds will continue to lose value over time as the futures contracts that make up the funds drop lower.

It's like buying and selling the same option over and over again. Even if the underlying stock eventually makes a big move, you've eaten up a lot of capital trading in and out, plus you've lost money from a declining time premium.

That creates a huge opportunity to short volatility when it periodically spikes. That's why this trade looks smart to me.

It looks stupid to me because shorting volatility could be a problem if I go short and volatility continues to rise. But since volatility charts look a lot like a heart monitor, the spikes up, while severe, tend to be brief and quickly unwind.

So let's look at the two ways I've taken advantage of volatility spikes to boost my returns during uncertain periods in the market.

#1: Selling Uncovered Calls on the VXX ETN and Other Related Products

The VXX ETN has lost more than 99 percent of its value since its inception in 2009. It undertracks the index. When the VIX is up 30 percent, the VXX might only shoot up 5 or 10 percent. It can have some big percentage moves upward in a day, but the long-term trend is down. Since the fund's very design ensures it will continually lose value over time, selling uncovered calls on the VXX during a volatility spike can lead to huge profits.

During these spikes, I've waited until the VIX is at least at 30. Then I've found options at least six months out with a strike price another 30 percent or so higher than what the VIX is trading at. Six months is more than enough time for volatility to subside, and if it doesn't, I have some wiggle room in terms of the shares rising further if I'm getting into the trade early.

But selling uncovered calls is absurdly risky. That's why these trades are probably the stupidest thing I've ever done to make money. If the underlying index rises enough, I may be on the hook for the calls. If I sell a $40 call on the VXX and it rises to $50 at expiration, I'm on the hook for $10 per share. Since I'm probably making $4 or $5 for selling the calls in the first place, I've turned a sizeable gain into a sizeable loss. While I think the returns are better using this strategy compared to the second strategy, it's only because of this higher risk—and one that could be terminal to any investor.

#2: Buying Puts When VIX Is High

This simpler way to trade volatility is to buy put options on the VXX ETN and related products when volatility is spiking. Again, I'm waiting for the VIX to pop past 30, only in this case, I'm looking to buy put options six months or so out from the present and at least 25 percent below the fund's current price. I'm not looking to hold the trade to expiration but rather to cash out after the VIX starts slipping back to its average price in the 20 range or when I've at least doubled my position.

This takes a lot of risk out of shorting volatility. When you buy an option, the money you put into a trade is the most you can lose. When that's it, even a small position doubling can make a major difference in your investment returns over time.

Here's how I see these volatility trades through the lens of our three investment criteria:

Safe: I don't believe that these trades are entirely safe from a day-to-day perspective. Over a few months, they likely will be. After all, whatever's bothering the market now tends to give way in a few weeks to a new narrative. Plus, given where volatility has been trading on average in recent years, I've waited for the VIX to spike up to at least 30 before I start to go hunting for short trades. That cuts the risk down considerably. Given that the VIX's long-term average is between 17 and 20, a VIX reading of 30 means that I'm starting to go short just as volatility is getting to be 50 percent above normal.

That's meant fewer and fewer opportunities to make these trades in the past few years. The last real opportunity was in February 2016 as I write, and in the summer of 2015, the VIX briefly shot up to 50 even though the overall market wasn't suffering that much. I anticipate anywhere from one to four spikes in volatility in a given year, so there's a lot of patience involved in waiting for those moments.

And even when there is a spike, it might not go up as much as I'd like. Again, given the risks of shorting volatility, I'm going to wait for a VIX reading of at least 30; 25 or even 28 just won't do. While I'm more flexible with other trades, if the VIX goes to 30, it might not stop until it hits 40 or 50. As soon as I start lowering my standards there, there's no telling what that will do to my returns on these trades.

I'm not the only one who's noticed and profited from this opportunity. And given how volatility-based funds have performed over the long term, I doubt that they'll survive in their current form. That's why, in future volatility spikes above 30, my ideal plan will be a much simpler one: to buy long-dated, out-of-the-money call options on the S&P 500 Index ETF (SPY). Since buying call options limits the maximum loss to whatever is put into a trade, there's less of a risk of losing money compared to selling uncovered call options.

Debt-Free: While these trades have been consistently profitable for me, solvency is my biggest concern. After all, in a 2008-style financial meltdown, where the VIX shoots up to 70 (or perhaps higher), shorting volatility at 30 won't just be a bad trade, it could be a real portfolio killer.

That's why I've shifted from the endless risk of selling uncovered call options to buying put options instead. And it's why I'm looking beyond pure-volatility trades for future spikes in the VIX so that I can better profit without having to deal with such a leveraged and challenging product to understand. By shifting to more understandable investments, like S&P 500 options, I know what I'm getting into. I'm simply using the VIX the way Wall Street traders do: as the market's fear indicator.

Even with the potential returns of this investment, given the huge daily moves involved, I've only used it in a trading account designed for my more bizarre ideas. It's not something you can do with a retirement account, nor is it something you'd want to do with a cash account where you know you'll need the money. The way I see it, trading volatility is one of the biggest speculations you can make, even if you're looking to short on one of its brief and periodic spikes upward. When volatility does spike, chances are you'll see your more conservative investments sell off as well. Just recognize that a volatility spike is a sign of an emerging buying opportunity, not a reason to panic out of your core trades. It also means it's time to bet on things calming down.

Rich: This trade has helped build wealth for one reason: the risk involved. When markets are selling off and fear spikes high, sometimes the biggest fear is that things will get worse. Historically, that happens only rarely. And even if there is a bear market, those tend to last 12–18 months at their worst. By waiting for those brief periods of time where volatility is trading at a much higher level than normal, the options premiums on shorting volatility-backed products are at their best.

Going forward, I don't think these trades will be as easy in the future. Volatility products are consistent long-term money losers. Furthermore, interest in volatility as a trade sprung up with the financial crisis. As that crisis becomes a distant memory, so has interest in trading these products.

In hindsight, these trades have been a great way to consistently build wealth—provided that we wait for an appropriate jump in volatility first. It's impossible to know when volatility will spike or by how much. But I have a plan in place to deal with these sudden but inevitable market fears and take advantage of them. That's the most important way to view these trades—even the more conservative ones like buying S&P 500 calls on a big enough jump in volatility.

PART IV

COMPLEX OPPORTUNITIES

Investing isn't always as neat as buying low and selling high. A lot can happen along the way, and being able to adapt to those trends is critical to improving investment returns. Once you've mastered the basics of investing and are looking for something more bizarre, chances are you'll be able to find it.

To me, a complex opportunity is one that doesn't fit into the other categories. It may involve something outside the traditional market as a means of profiting. Or it might mean finding a way to turn a losing trade into a winning one. Finally, this category also includes companies that are so complex that investing in them just might end up costing you nearly all your investment when things don't go right—and how to avoid making the same mistake I once did.

CHAPTER 15

Herbalife

Sneaking in Profits during a Battle of the Billionaires

OFTEN TIMES, A TRADE COMES down to a binary outcome. Either one event will happen or it won't. For instance, a pharmaceutical company's shares may wildly rise upon FDA approval for a promising drug. But if that drug isn't approved, shares might fall instead. That's a binary event.

On its face, that may sound a bit like a roll of the dice rather than a prudent speculation. However, every situation is different. And many times, the company facing a binary event may be an ongoing concern in any case; it's simply a question of whether shares will rise first or fall before eventually heading higher.

In the past few years, one of the most high-profile binary outcomes has been revolving around the nutrition company **Herbalife (HLF)**. It's been a high-stakes battle involving two well-known investment billionaires. It's only a matter of time before you get the Hollywood version, but here's the summary of what's been going on:

In 2013, hedge fund billionaire Bill Ackman of Pershing Square Capital publicly disclosed a massive short position in the company. Ackman's thesis that the company, which relies on multilevel marketing (MLM) as a business model, wasn't just unsustainable. It was an outright fraud. Ackman believed that the company's proper price was zero.

Another billionaire, Carl Icahn, took the opposite side, publicly declaring support for the company and buying up millions of shares. While the company used the MLM model to operate, it still sold real goods to real people and had real demands. The notion that the company was a fraud seemed ridiculous.[1]

That's the binary outcome. If Icahn was right, shares had been unfairly punished by Ackman's large short position and his public statements about the company being worth zero. If Ackman was right, the company was more than just overvalued and shorting shares represented a huge—and rare—opportunity on the short side.

Usually, a trade like this would have played out rather quickly. But Ackman didn't just stop with a low-cost public relations campaign. He spent millions to support his view that the company was a fraud. Despite his attempts to get numerous investigations started, only the Federal Trade Commission (FTC) decided to investigate the company regarding promises made to recruits in the MLM space.

My thought was that the company wasn't a fraud. If it was, it would mean that other companies also operating as multilevel-marketing organizations would also be considered fraudulent. But government agencies had ruled in the past that these companies were fine.[2] While it's an unusual way to operate, it's not illegal. That meant that any major drop in Herbalife prices would make the shares worth buying.

I didn't enter the picture until early 2015 as events continued to play out. Shares had spent several years gyrating between $30 and $70 as the saga unfolded. And in early 2015, they were back into the mid-$30s once again. Using the strategy of selling put options, I managed to acquire a few hundred shares at a cost near $30. Because of the huge binary event surrounding the company, the options premiums were huge, so selling puts was the most logical way to enter into this trade.

The timing proved fortunate. By August, shares had shrugged off the recent slump and had soared to $60. At that price, with nearly a clean double on my hand, writing covered calls on the stock was the next logical step. After all, as long as the market was pricing a binary event and the stock was so volatile on a daily basis, the options premiums were huge. Selling covered call options allowed me to recover more than 15 percent of my original stake within six months of buying shares. That's a huge out-sized options return and a sign that, no matter what happened to the company, I'd be generating substantial income off the trade even though the common shares paid no dividend.

Shares have since traded between the high $40s and high $60s. As I write in early 2017, I've managed to sell covered call options a number of times on shares without having them get called away. As a result, I'm making more than 20 percent per year out of this position, which is still trading at a substantially higher level than where I bought shares. Even better, in mid-2016, the FTC announced their ruling, clearing the company of any wrongdoing. While that made for a great short-term boost in shares, what matters going forward is how the company performs operationally.

As I write, the company has beaten earnings estimates in all four quarters of the past year. While there are some changes to the company's business model to avoid further government concerns and the company did have to pay a fine to the FTC as a cost of doing business, the company continues to perform well overseas where the multilevel-marketing structure isn't as big of a concern.[3]

Markets offer a few opportunities for binary events every year. Only a very few attract public attention and the investments of billionaires on both sides of the trade. Most won't. But if you can look past the headlines and the heated views coming from traders on both sides, you just might be able to find a good trading opportunity.

On its face, the trade sounds like a bit of luck was involved. I won't lie to you—events could have gone the other way. But if the FTC had shut down Herbalife's US operations, it still wouldn't have been that bad, especially with my low-cost basis.

This is a particularly complicated trade, so let's take a little more time to run it through our three criteria to show why it's worked out so profitably thus far:

Safe: On the face of it, the trade looked risky. In early 2015, you had a company that was being loudly and publicly shorted by a billionaire investor armed with a media team and 100-plus-page PowerPoint presentations on why the company was doomed. But on the other side of the trade, you had one billionaire who was publicly in favor of the stock and a few other wealthy folks who were also taking advantage of the bad public relations in the short term to buy up shares. The fundamentals were sound.

The real kicker that made this a safe trade, however, was the fact that the company operates around the world in dozens of countries. While the United States single-handedly makes up around 20 percent of the company's income, the flip side of that proposition is that 80 percent of the company's income comes from other countries. Shares had already lost nearly half their value after the short-side attack was mounted by Ackman. So from an operational standpoint, which is what truly matters for investing over the long term, shares had been unfairly beaten down.

What's more, other governments had already looked into Herbalife and other companies operating under the MLM model. They had been given a clean bill of health. While some countries and cultures do things a little differently, local laws and regulations mean that Herbalife operates a little differently in some countries than in others. That's normal for just about any industry. The prospect of the company being worth shorting to zero, when considering the company's international scale and sales, had now become simply absurd.

Because the underlying company looked safe, and because shares had sold off far more than the company would lose being shut down in one country, the safety of the trade appeared overwhelming. As a trade, the only thing about it I didn't like was that buying shares outright would produce no income. So the way around that was to sell put options and, having been put during a period of maximum pessimism in Herbalife shares, turn around and sell covered calls once I had generated some gains.

Debt-Free: As a trade, I was glad I wasn't on the short side. It's an expensive proposition. Ackman covered part of his short trade before I had bought, since shares had surged and he was underwater on the trade. He claimed that he had since moved toward using put options to short the company. But when you're buying put options and the price doesn't go down fast enough, you'll bleed out time premium. In any event, it's easy to get caught in financial quicksand on the short side, especially if you directly short shares and don't use options.

On the long side, I had a variety of ways to profit. By starting with selling put options, I could generate some income out of the cash I had set aside for this trade before I had even acquired a single share. Since I used cash-secured put options, where I had 100 percent of the cash available for the trade, I had no problem getting put shares of Herbalife. The put options did what they were designed to do: to pay me to wait to buy shares at a price I liked.

Given the volatility in those shares, I expected the trade to bounce around for a while. But shares rose quickly after my initial purchase. I was then faced with another challenge to staying out of financial trouble in the trade: What to do with those gains? While I could have quickly sold out, I felt there was still more upside to owning the shares.

However, because I had sold put options to enter into the trade, I owned shares in round lots of 100, which make it easy to turn around and sell covered call options now that the trade was up. So staying solvent on this trade meant taking on the "risk" of selling my shares at a profit, and getting a handsome income on the long side to do so as well.

In effect, because of the perceived "binary" outcome of this trade, there were a lot of strong feelings that shares were worth either far more or far less than where they were trading at any given time. In the options market, that translated into higher options premiums in both directions. My real value on this trade was in taking advantage of those fat premiums.

Rich: What made this trade for me is that it wasn't the typical binary trade. In fact, it's been a very dynamic trade. I took advantage of the stock's trading range to sell put options near the low point. I was put shares, something every put-seller should expect to occur every once in a while, even with a modest margin of safety in the trade.

The stock's quick jump within a few months of acquiring shares might have led most traders to take quick profits and run. But this was an investment that simply looked like a trade thanks to the short-term uncertainty of the FTC investigation and Bill Ackman's willingness to spend his clients' money talking down a stock he was shorting. The fundamentals of the company were strong, albeit somewhat depressed in the US market following the big and nasty public campaign Ackman was waging against the company.

But what truly made this trade wealth-creating was the ability to extract capital out of the trade with the covered call writing once shares had quickly doubled in value following the initial purchase. With Ackman and the FTC acting as an overhang, it was unlikely that shares, which I thought were worth perhaps as much as $85 if the company were free and clear, would rise past $70 given the current conditions. That made for an ideal strike price on the call options, which weren't that much higher.

Since the options market tends to look at a rising or falling stock and extrapolate that short-term trend out to infinity, the options premiums were great. The same thing happened when selling the put options initially. Shares had slid too far, too quickly, but the options market hadn't caught on to that fact. They were assuming the trend would continue. But even if the FTC had decided the company needed to be shut down in the United States, their international operations gave the company a minimum value of at least $35 per share. So selling put options with that strike price was sensible as the market had been unduly pessimistic.

The road to wealth is varied. One great trade can get you to your destination much more quickly, but a series of income-producing trades can provide a great way to do so as well.

This trade isn't over for me as I write. Eventually, the stock's fundamentals will take the stock to a new trading range—and likely a higher one. But I expect to get all of my initial capital out via options trades before that happens. That's a lesser-known, but just as valuable, road to wealth.

CHAPTER 16

Staying Solvent 101

Don't Put All Your Cash in One Trade

AS AN INVESTOR, STAYING SOLVENT is critical to your financial safety, especially the long-term preservation of your wealth. That should be obvious, but it bears repeating. After all, we often don't fully think about our portfolio as a whole or how a trade could work against us as we make it. That's why it's important to limit your trades and the overall size of your investments. And avoid trades that could put you on the hook—and get you stuck in debt. Most investors put their solvency at risk by making trades that are too large relative to the size of their overall portfolio.

When I first started investing in individual stocks, I split my money into two trades—a 50 percent stake in each. But the total sum was only a few thousand dollars, and I knew that I would be making regular contributions over time to quickly add additional cash. By the time I was taking profits on those trades, my account had swelled, largely because of new cash being added to the portfolio on a regular basis.

Today, I wouldn't put more than 10 percent of my money into a single trade. That way, in the unlikely (but not impossible) event that a trade works against me and goes to zero, the most my portfolio would lose on the whole would be 10 percent. The market often dips that much throughout a given year as stocks fluctuate, and it's a level that, while painful in the short term, can be easy to recover from.

I know some people who will put more of their money, up to 25 percent, into a single trade. Unless you have a very specific knowledge of the company involved, I wouldn't recommend it. There's simply too much solvency risk if that trade goes against you. This mostly applies to individual names and not a board fund that invests in multiple companies. Even with a 10 percent stake, a trade that works out in your favor will have a big impact on your overall portfolio in a way that doesn't risk a solvency problem and cause your portfolio to suffer a terminal loss.

But there are other ways to blow up your account that don't require that you directly trade stocks. I like to try new things as an investor. But one experiment put my solvency at short-term risk. While things eventually worked out well for me, it could have easily gone the other way.

By 2012, I was regularly using options to improve my investment returns. My favorite strategy involved selling put options—essentially getting paid a premium to take on the risk of being put shares of a company. While I generally liked the returns I could get 6-9 months out, I had also started to look at the weekly options of search engine giant **Google (GOOG, now named Alphabet)**.

The rationale was simple. Here was a big, giant industry leader. There was no risk of a competitor, at least one that could derail a weekly trade. It was stable and less susceptible to big moves like other tech companies that had different expectations from Wall Street—like how Apple's (AAPL) iPhone sales were doing each quarter. No, the company just quietly and consistently made money, usually beating expectations in the process.

So I started a weekly put-selling trading plan. It was pretty simple, really: I'd sell a put on a Monday with an expiration date on the following Friday, and given the price that Google shares traded at, I could make around $150 to $200 per week selling slightly out-of-the-money put options. The catch was that Google shares traded around $600. So it tied up my entire cash stake of around $60,000 in the portfolio to sell just one contract. But I would be on track to make around 13 percent per year, a far better use of my cash than letting it sit around earning next to nothing.

Of course, there's a reason the annual potential return looked so high: there was a risk that shares would drop below the strike price I was using. On October 18, 2012, Google didn't just report surprisingly lower-than-expected earnings. The earnings were so bad they had been leaked ahead of time![1]

Shares dropped 8 percent, putting the trade well in-the-money. The decision was then to keep the option and be put the shares, or close out the trade at a sizeable loss several times the income I had expected to make.

Many traders might have seen their position shift against them quickly and hit the panic button, closing out the trade at any price. But as investors, we make our money in part by keeping our cool during big, unexpected market moves, so I took a few minutes to analyze the leaked earnings. Yes, the numbers didn't look so good, and there was a big headline miss. But despite the bad overall numbers, things didn't look so bad once you got past the headline and drilled down into the actual business itself. The core business—its search engine platform, a brand likely stronger now than Coca-Cola (KO), Harley (HOG) or Disney (DIS)—seemed to be doing fine. It was the struggling Motorola division that was holding things back, at least for the moment.[2]

Although I knew it would use up nearly all of my cash, it made more sense to be put the shares instead of panicking and closing out at a loss. And while Google doesn't pay a dividend, I knew the tech giant's fortunes would change and that Mr. Market's opinion of the stock would likewise adjust—possibly rapidly. While things looked immediately bad for my portfolio due to the decline and how much of it was now concentrated in one stock, I believed that shares would eventually turn themselves around. The fundamentals were fine. Most Google investors knew the Motorola division was troublesome. It was really about the leaked earnings numbers before the market closed.

Following the market close on Friday, the option was exercised and I was put shares. Because the put option was at-the-money before the drop, I was down in dollar terms almost exactly as much as the option had gone down. But now I wasn't an options trader; I was long the stock, and time was on my side. It took a few months for the shares to begin to turn and another few rounds of earnings seasons for the market to see past the damaging effect of the leak and start to trend higher. While dividend payments would have at least provided some return of capital, Google's lack of a dividend meant sticking through the day-to-day swings.

But things turned around with a vengeance, and within a year and a half, in March 2014, shares had nearly doubled and were looking to split two-for-one to get the price back down. At that point, an immediate loss had been turned around into a sizeable gain. It made sense, given the company's powerful rally, to sell half the stake. When you get your original money back, you're like a player at the casino playing with the houses' money. It means you can take some risks or let a good ride continue to make its run.

That's when it became an income-themed trade again. Instead of selling put options on the remaining stake, however, I could now sell covered call options on the trade. That was a much better position to be in, since I'd either get called away and substantially increase my cash holdings, or I wouldn't get called away and I'd get to keep a small premium each week. I managed to collect premiums for a few weeks before the rising share price meant I was finally called away. But it was one amazing ride. I had more than doubled my money in less than 18 months out of a trade that was initially designed to boost my cash returns in my options trading portfolio. It's not the kind of trade I intended to make, but it proved to be a good reminder of the need to keep an eye on the size of your trade . . . it may often be a bigger part of your portfolio than it seems at first!

This trade is an example of my own imperfection as an investor, as well as how the market doesn't always move the way you expect it to. While I didn't lose money on the trade, I could have. But selling put options on Google, a company with a strong brand, meant that it would have been difficult to lose money over time, even in the midst of short-term fears.

That's the beauty of sticking to high-quality investments, whether you're using stocks, options, or investing in something else: it means that you'll likely come out ahead so long as you have patience and don't give in to fear.

Here are my thoughts running the trade through our three filters:

Safe: I failed the safety test when selling put options on Google each week. I sold options just barely below the strike price. That made sense considering that the company tended to move 1–2 percent day to day. But I didn't have enough of a margin of safety for a whopping 8 percent decline. While such declines were unlikely in Google shares, they weren't impossible. And during earnings season or a market panic, many stocks that are usually calm on a daily basis also start to make bigger swings up or down depending on the news.

In the second part of the trade, however, things became far safer. Once shares split two-for-one after nearly doubling, I was able to get my original capital out of the trade. The shares I kept essentially allowed me to play with the houses' money. What's more, what had started as a risky income trade became a safe income trade. Covered call options, where you already own the underlying shares, are less likely to suddenly suck up your capital compared to being put shares instead.

Debt-Free: I very nearly failed the financial safety test on this particular trade as well. I was putting nearly all the cash in my options trading account into one company. While the annualized returns for that pile of cash looked great, it meant that if things went wrong, all that cash would be tied up. My original plan was to keep an eye on the trade from week to week and simply let the option expire without writing a new put option if I found a better investment opportunity for the cash. That didn't pan out at all.

In the second part of the trade, however, things turned around and there was plenty of solvency. I was able to take a massive amount of money out after shares split and still be partially in the trade.

At no time did I feel the need to close out the trade while it was a loss in order to raise cash. While the trade ended up using most of my capital, I didn't require the cash for other trades at the time. It looked like the best trade to make for the moment. Since I don't plan on retiring or otherwise using the money in that account for anything other than making trades, there was no need for the cash elsewhere and no need to panic over the short-term. In short, I had no real fear about the trade failing to pan out. It would just take time.

Rich: I think this trade did work to make me rich in both parts. In the first part, selling put options, I was able to increase my portfolio income in a company I was willing to be put shares of at that price. Given Google's strength, however, it simply seemed unlikely that the trade would end up going in-the-money and requiring me to buy shares.

However, the second part of the trade dramatically upped the wealth potential. Being long shares as they substantially rise meant a huge and unexpected capital gain. Following the two-for-one split, I could again sell weekly options to get back to earning weekly income, only this time on the call option side.

CHAPTER 17

Homestyle Investing

Turning Your Next Home into a Moneymaker

THIS ISN'T A TRADE AS far as most people are concerned, but many *do* think of homeownership as an investment. To some extent, I agree. When you buy in the right place (location, location, location) and at the right time, you can significantly offset your housing costs through price appreciation, as I'll show below. But as with investing in any stock, it will still come down to discipline and patience in order to make money in real estate.

I've been fortunate on that front. For the past seven years, I've had my home appreciate $90,000. That's not bad for a three-bedroom, two-bathroom suburban Florida home that I bought as a foreclosure. But here's the kicker: since I only put down a net amount of $1,000, my return as I write is a staggering 90-fold return on my money. What's more, I've had a place to hang my hat in the meantime.

I'll get into the specific math as we look at this trade through the lens of our safe, debt-free, and rich criteria. But it's important to remember that real estate often represents the biggest asset that anyone will ever own. It's an area where people will often ask my opinion, even though I'm really a stock guy first. And as a house is also often a *home*, there can be a lot more emotion involved compared to investing in stocks. That's why it's a bit of a contentious claim that real estate makes a good investment: Some view a home as an investment. Some don't. It can depend a lot on how long you've lived there, the price appreciation, and the general mood of the economy. Someone who's lived in the same home for 40 years has likely not only paid off a mortgage but seen fantastic price appreciation along the way if they live in a market like San Francisco, San Diego, Miami, or Washington DC. Residents in other states might have had poorer results. That's to be expected for an asset that all comes down to location, location, location.

But even those fast-moving markets have their slow periods. As I write, the once red-hot Bay Area in California is slowing. Top of the line New York City apartment prices are being reduced.[1] The slow periods are the time to buy. As with buying shares of an unloved company, the important factor is to let the pessimism as others pique your interest.

I view my home as both a place to live *and* an investment. Why? Because I had the combination of a great price and a great location, and I waited until the housing market was so out-of-favor as an investment that by the time Uncle Sam and my former landlord were done handing me money, I only had to put $1,000 down.

How? Because the US government wants me to be a homeowner. It wants you to be a homeowner too. In fact, the government pretty much wants everyone to be a homeowner, to the point where you can get some fantastic deals on real estate that you just can't get with stocks.

For instance, with my current home, I qualified as a first-time homebuyer. That means that I qualified for a Federal Housing Administration (FHA) loan. The beauty of that was, instead of having to put down the traditional 20 percent equity on a home purchase, I only had to put down 3.5 percent of the purchase price.

That helped lower the amount of money I had to pay out of pocket, although it also meant that I needed to pay more monthly in the form of private mortgage insurance (PMI). It was a worthwhile trade-off at the time, but I was glad to be rid of the PMI once I was able to refinance with a more traditional 20 percent equity loan.

Next, I bought in late 2009, when the government, in the interest of propping up the failing real estate market, was offering a first-time homebuyer tax credit of $8,000. I qualified. Although I wouldn't see that money until after my tax return processed in 2010, that created a huge incentive to buy now. The only problem was, after the program ended, so did that incentive to buy, and home sales and prices remained weak for a few years after that.

Third, owning a home made more sense than renting. What I was paying a landlord monthly, I was now paying a bank, but at the end of 30 years, I would own the home free and clear, whereas after 30 years of renting, the landlord would still own the property. Sure, maintenance and repairs would now be on me. But so would the ability to better customize my living space. That's a trade-off worth making.

Finally, thanks to the timing, I was able to buy the home for just a bit less than the replacement cost. In other words, it would have been more costly to buy a similar-sized lot and build a similar-sized home than it would be to buy this existing home. And looking through the real estate records, the home had last traded hands for over $300,000 during the housing bubble. I was buying at over a 50 percent discount compared to that peak price. For any stock that's not going out of business, that's a great bargain. In real estate, that kind of deal will only come around a handful of times.

While I'm pleased with the home equity, particularly compared to how little I initially had to put in, I didn't make that sizeable return overnight. Heck, I didn't even see any price appreciation in my home until after I had lived there nearly four years. It's not like owning an investment like a stock where the price is regularly updated throughout the day. Rather, it's more of a month-to-month or even quarterly view that shows price trends in a housing market. That's OK; after all, you need somewhere to live in the meantime!

If you own or want to own a house to live in for the rest of your life, then how much money you can make off of it as an investment really doesn't apply. That means you can ignore the housing market's ups and downs. That's a great way to think of the ultimate buy-and-hold investment—one that can be left for the kids to inherit.

However you view real estate, it can be part of your portfolio. Besides having a place to live, real estate investment trusts (REITs) offer a way to benefit from cash-producing real estate. These REITs pay higher dividends than common stocks and can allow you to play landlord without the hassle of having to take 3 a.m. calls for broken pipes or other annoyances. This is also a great way to get in and out of a real estate investment quickly and without high commissions. That's a win-win if you're looking to put your capital to work, not yourself to work as a landlord.

As always, let's take a look and see how buying a home at the right time led to a safe, debt-free, and rich outcome:

Safe: This investment seemed safe at the time for a few reasons. First was the cash situation. With a first-time homebuyer tax credit, the end of renting, and the return of my security deposit, I didn't have to put that much money into the home. In the event of another housing market crash, I could have walked away with little financial loss.

Second, I was buying a foreclosed home. It needed a lot of work, but as a result, the value was great in terms of price to square feet for the zip code at the time. It also meant that my monthly mortgage payment was comparable to what I was paying in rent at the time on a two-bedroom condo. Only now, I'd be building equity in a home and I wouldn't have to face annual increases in rent. So in terms of cash flow, while there might be some unpredictable expenses related to homeownership, I would have far more control compared to renting.

Debt-Free: I'll be completely honest here. This is, hands down, the least solvent trade you could ever make. It involves taking on considerable debt and goes against the debt-free lifestyle that I live when it comes to my stock investments. It's also partly why some people view investing in real estate as risky. There's no solvency here. I can't sell off part of the property a little bit at a time like I can sell off a stake in shares of stocks. It's also unlikely you'll sell the property in a day—unless you're willing to take a huge hit on price.

In addition to being insolvent, there are high costs to getting in and out of real estate. You'll typically spend 6 percent or so in commissions to a real estate agent and hundreds of dollars on inspections and small repairs on the way out once you do get an offer. It's enough to make a profitable real estate investment on paper turn into a money pit in reality.

In my personal case, which might not mirror all real estate markets right now, I am somewhat fortunate. Homes in my neighborhood, as I write, don't sit on the market for too long. And prices are still near their post–housing bubble highs. While I might not be able to sell instantly like a stock, I've selected a place to live that has a lot of solid characteristics that folks are looking for: a good location, plenty of amenities, relatively low costs, and so on.

Rich: What made buying a home most appealing to me was the low out-of-pocket cost at the time I bought. Again, this is specific to me, but I waited until Uncle Sam was willing to basically just give me a house. With the first-time homebuyer tax credit of $8,000, the $10,000 that I needed to put down on my home was reduced to $2,000. And since I was no longer renting, I received my $1,000 security deposit back, making the net cost on my home a modest $1,000.

Remember, this was in 2009, at the bottom of the real estate market. Homes in my neighborhood didn't appreciate right away. It took substantial time for the market to start trending upward—nearly four years after I had bought. But my costs stayed the same rather than increasing, as the rent would have. By the time prices did start appreciating, I had been able to do most of the major repair work without getting financially overextended. I was even able to refinance after the price rose enough to get rid of the monthly private mortgage insurance (PMI), a needless expense.

Conclusion

To make a long story short, some people see their home as a home. But it can be a potential investment too, if you're willing to look at it that way and buy right. We might get another opportunity to buy a home with major government inducements like the first-time homebuyers tax credit back in 2009, but such opportunities will be rare. Even without it, real estate can offer tremendous returns if you're patient. And that's the key—unlike stocks, you'll need to be patient!

One final word: As I write, interest rates are continuing to be ratcheted up from their 40-year lows.[2] As these rates rise, so will mortgage rates. If you own a home or are looking to own a home, make sure you're in a fixed-rate mortgage. When rates go up, variable-rate mortgages will go up as well, increasing your monthly payments. If all you want to do with real estate is own your dream home, make sure your costs stay the same so that you don't have to deal with any unexpected rises. After all, insurance and taxes will probably rise over time as well.

Some people don't mind holding a mortgage, but some do. While mortgages can be financed anywhere from 15 to 40 years, I'd still go with the 30-year mortgage. If you're looking to pay that down faster, simply make extra principal payments every month. This strategy gives you some wiggle room if you face a cash shortage or temporarily find yourself out of work: you can simply stop making the extra payments until you can afford to again.

CHAPTER 18

Nobody Bats 1000

Lessons Learned from a Big Loss
during the Financial Crisis

IF YOU'RE DOING YOUR JOB well as an investor and thinking about the possible downside of an investment before you get in, the upside will tend to take care of itself. Then the biggest challenge becomes when to sell. Sometimes that may seem early or late depending on circumstances, but by selling when you're up, you guarantee profits.

But nobody's perfect. You'll have investment losses from time to time. That's OK. It's how you handle those losses—and what you learn from them—that shows your mettle as an investor.

Many stocks might drop below your entry price, and stay there for weeks, months, or even years before they turn around. I don't mind holding a stock at a loss from where I officially bought shares for a few reasons. First, if the fundamental premise doesn't change, it means that I'll still likely be right over time. I'm not looking to buy shares of a company on Monday and sell on Friday. If I were, I'd make a wager with an options trade. For any real investment, I need at least one year for the idea to unfold, possibly more. If it's a great company at a great price with a fantastic long-term track record, my holding period can be indefinite.

Second, if shares drop enough, and if the premise for owning the investment is still there, I can buy more shares. That allows me to lower my cost basis, so that when things do turn around and work out well, I can get to profitability at a lower price. That's how you turn a short-term loss into a long-term win!

Finally, if I need to offset my gains, I can sell the loss for the tax write-off at the end of one year and buy it back 31 days later at the start of another year. That allows me to take advantage of the government's willingness to let me write off up to $3,000 in investment losses against my income every year.

I'd say most market declines cause temporary losses that can be mitigated in time. However, capitalism is dynamic. Some companies end up going through tough times that they can't recover from. Avoiding these types of situations is critical to your investment returns. After all, if you lose 100 percent of the money you put into a trade, it can't compound. When your money isn't making money for you but is instead destroyed, something's gone terribly amiss.

That brings us to my biggest screw-up to date. I had one terminal loss in my investment portfolio during the financial crisis. On the one hand, that makes it sound like I have gotten off easily, but on the other hand, I should have had more skepticism going into the trade. While I still approached the trade with a view of what could go wrong, the scale of the financial crisis ended up taking me by surprise on this position.

The trade was in the now-defunct Thornburg Mortgage. It was a position I had started adding back in 2005, and it was on its way to becoming a core income holding for my portfolio, at least until Mr. Market's panic during the financial crisis led to other plans.

At one point the largest publicly traded company out of New Mexico, the company was a mortgage REIT focused on high-end investors. While federal guarantees for mortgages cut off after certain amounts, Thornburg had stepped in the higher-end market. The rise of the McMansion era and homes valued more than $550,000 throughout the market needed servicing, and Thornburg had a system that worked well until the crisis.

Like any lender, Thornburg was looking at someone's ability to pay, as well as the value of the underlying home. By focusing on investing in properties where someone had a high-paying job, the company believed that they'd fare as well, if not better than, lower-end mortgage providers.

But they were working without a government net that lenders on less expensive properties had. The outbreak of the financial crisis led to lost jobs, missed mortgage payments, and thus missed cash flow. That led to a liquidity crisis in the company, as also happened to other lenders at the time. The company cut, then eliminated, its massive double-digit dividend.

Things got worse. Without liquidity to service its existing portfolio, and with that portfolio collapsing rapidly in value, shares collapsed within a matter of days in 2008.

In fairness, the issues surrounding Thornburg—and other financial companies at the time—were part of a generational aberration. While we'll continue to face crises again as investors, few, if any, in our lifetime will match the speed and severity of the Great Recession of 2007–9.

While I was taking a dive in Thornburg, the rest of my portfolio remained cash-heavy. That's because there were few opportunities that made sense. The values that I had been able to find in the market weren't there anymore. And the overall market sentiment had gone from being unduly bullish to more cautious. At the time, I was nearly completely out of the commodity space as a result. Nearly everything had run up and there were no opportunities there. But there weren't as many opportunities in individual stocks in other sectors either.

As a result, Thornburg looked *relatively* sensible as an investment. As a REIT, the real focus was on the dividends, not the day-to-day performance. Under most market conditions, it would have made sense to hold on to shares, collect the dividends, and wait for the market to recover. But given the housing-centric nature of the crisis, Thornburg's inability to get cash when it needed it the most ended up making for a terminal loss.

With the benefit of hindsight, we can see how the company fared using our three investment criteria:

Safe: As with many other financial companies, Thornburg Mortgage appeared safe. Even before the crisis, the financial sector was a highly regulated space. But Thornburg decided to operate outside the government-guaranteed part of the market. In hindsight, this should have been a red flag.

What's more, as a mortgage REIT, the company was one of the most leveraged firms on the market. They made good money, but on a narrow spread between their borrowing costs and what they were charging for mortgages. As a result of that leverage, it only took a tiny move in the housing market to make sizeable trouble for the company.

Leverage isn't always a problem. When used correctly, it's a useful tool for improving your investment returns. Buying a call option, for example, is a form of leverage. And while you can lose money options trading, you also know your downside when buying an option—the entire price you paid. Buying companies that use leverage instead shifts the burden of using that leverage responsibly.

When things are going well, it behooves a company to increase leverage to further improve their returns. What makes a good investment then is a company that refrains from getting as leveraged as possible and focuses on trying to improve its profitability in other ways as a result.

Debt-Free: On its face, the company was solvent . . . until it wasn't. The company had plenty of money to finance operations and was able to borrow short term as needed to meet cash-flow needs. Like most mortgage REITs, Thornburg had massive debt, but was financed at a rate that didn't pose a problem under most financial conditions. But conditions changed, and the company's massive debt became, to some extent, my problem as well as a result. It goes to show that debt, even if you're not the direct holder, can be dangerous.

As an investor, the REIT status was a goldmine. It allowed the company to pay out a generous dividend, and as a result, I was able to keep about 20 percent of the money I had put in. However, by the time I was able to get out of shares, it was at a steep loss.

One factor regarding solvency is that of liquidity. That's your ability to get out of a trade quickly and without moving the market too much. If you own a huge amount of shares, you'll want to sell your stake in pieces so that the market can digest it. If you own a small-cap company, even a few hundred shares can move the market.

During the financial crisis, the issue was *illiquidity*. That's when the markets were so uncertain of what many stocks were worth (including nonfinancial stocks during the autumn of 2008 during the worst of it) that they traded with wild moves. The stock market had its biggest point moves down during the crisis—but also some of its biggest up moves due to the uncertainty. To some extent, those moves also reflect a lack of liquidity. When buyers started coming into the market, they moved it too far in the other direction!

The best thing to do, if you can, is take advantage of the big down moves to buy solvent companies during those periods. If you've done your job right, you'll have avoided companies that face terminal losses, like Thornburg, along the way.

This lack of liquidity is something to watch out for. If you do your job right as an investor, you'll get out of problematic stocks before that becomes an issue. But sometimes you can end up getting swept up in the fervor of markets. If the market for common shares has become illiquid, chances are the company itself couldn't get short-term financing if it needed it. If that poses a problem for a position in your portfolio, you should be prepared to sell at the first sign of trouble to avoid this particular issue.

Rich: This trade could have made me rich. A lot of trades can make your rich, but most don't. In the case of Thornburg, the market's liquidity dried up and the company couldn't get the cash it needed to get it over the hump and stay in business. Some changes before or during the financial crisis could have helped. The biggest problem was buying into a company that didn't fit with the government's guarantees as many other competitors did.

While I did get some money out of the trade via dividends and managed to sell out before the company went officially bankrupt in early 2009, the loss was staggering. That it was not a complete loss shows the value of owning dividend-paying firms. It's also a warning that the path to riches isn't always with highly leveraged companies. These companies do fine most of the time, but when markets sour, as they'll periodically do, the big and fast gains can quickly become losses.

The only real "wealth" I've gotten from this trade was that I now know to avoid overly leveraged companies. The mortgage REITs in particular are typically some of the most leveraged companies on the market at any time. Usually, their debt load shouldn't be an issue. But nonmortgage REITs use lower levels of debt. It's better to collect a safe 6 percent yield in a company owning the underlying buildings than in a lender that can pay 10 percent until trouble strikes.

It's the biggest investment loss I've known, and I earned it by buying into a company whose past performance couldn't prepare it for the biggest market blowup since the Great Depression. With hindsight, I could have avoided it—and even significantly profited from the financial crisis. But there's also a store of wealth in making a mistake and learning from it . . . and sharing my mistake with others so that they can learn from it too.

The path to wealth isn't just in making money in stocks most of the time. Avoiding big losses prevents you from digging yourself into a financial hole and having to dig your way out before your wealth can start compounding again. To avoid terminal losses in your portfolio, avoid overly leveraged companies. Sell out of highly leveraged companies at the first sign of trouble. Don't let the allure of a big dividend be the final consideration for buying a high-yielding stock.

Finally, remember that many companies *aren't* likely to become terminal losses like Thornburg Mortgage. Most of the time when stocks are dropping, what's needed most is the patience to see the latest decline through and the fortitude to pick up shares of quality names when they're cheap enough.

CONCLUSION AND APPENDICES

Armed with these case studies, you should have a much better idea of how to invest compared to reading a dry, boring book about analyzing charts or financial statements. Markets are living, breathing things, and understanding what's going on and where the opportunities are makes a lot more sense.

But in just looking at these case studies, we've glossed over a few ideas that bear covering. First, if you've read through these case studies and you're somehow turned off to the idea of trading, I've created a model portfolio you can follow instead of jumping into and out of investment ideas. I call it the "lazy way out," but hey, as long as you're still investing, you should do well with this model portfolio over time.

I've also included a few quick notes on personal finance to maximize your returns in the most tax-efficient way possible. Everyone's financial situation is different, so if you need more advice, you'll want to talk to your accountant.

I've also included a few thoughts I have on the government and the role it can play in either improving or hurting your investment returns. That's an issue that can come up more often than it seems in investing.

Finally, we end with a simple investment checklist. It's a short version of what I use when I find a promising trading opportunity. I want to make sure that I understand what I'm putting my money into—and I want you to have that same advantage.

The Lazy Way Out

*A Model Portfolio to Take Advantage
of Market Opportunities*

MOST PEOPLE DON'T HAVE THE time, effort, or energy to responsibly position and monitor their investments every time things change. I get it. People also flock to the idea of being able to "set and forget" their investments. I can understand the appeal. It's a far cry from the case studies that I've presented throughout this book, although it does sound a lot like what I try to do with core trades in my portfolio.

Laziness can be great—and when done right, most investing is simply that. It truly is an exercise in patience. You *can* be a lazy investor. But it means waiting for the price of an asset to come down to an acceptable purchase price or waiting for an investment to appreciate in price enough to justify selling. By foregoing buying and selling, you can focus on a few key assets that you know and understand well. You'll also avoid brokerage fees and short-term tax considerations. Whether you're the kind of person who wants to make 10 trades before grabbing your morning coffee or whether 10 trades per decade is more your style, laziness *can* pay off.

Indeed, the bulk of an investment portfolio should, over time, favor assets that can be held indefinitely. This saves on brokerage fees and taxes, simplifies estate planning, and makes it easier to keep tabs on your portfolio, even when your time is best spent elsewhere.

That's where this sample portfolio comes in. I've based it loosely off of the annual portfolio review that I perform with my family around the holidays. The goal is simple: construct a portfolio that can benefit from the trends that are most likely to occur over the next several years while still keeping an eye on downside risk. In other words, grow wealth without getting blown up by the markets if there's another big crash.

The Passive Investor Portfolio at a Glance

Fair warning, the portfolio I'm about to outline can't predict any seismic changes in the economy that may occur. Substantial changes may be necessary as new economic information presents itself. This portfolio also can't take into consideration your current or future investment needs, nor your tolerance for risk.

This breakdown is based on how I would invest for someone today with the caveat that investors shouldn't cash out for at least three years. It's based on the view that there is a low risk of deflation over the next few years and that inflation will likely rise, but still be moderate at best over time. With the Federal Reserve gradually increasing interest rates as I write, but with rates still near historic lows and below 1 percent, there's room for either case to play out.

Again, for passive investors, this portfolio allocation should emphasize the trends most likely to occur over the next few years, while also being positioned to avoid market dangers that may lurk along the way. Specific investment ideas for each category have already been discussed in their respective chapters earlier in this book. Even if you're a lazy investor, you will still have to do some homework to find investments that can perform well over the long term and fit your risk parameters so you can profit and sleep well at night.

Here's how I would set up a portfolio today for a passive investor:

·   40 Percent: Dividend Growth, "Core Portfolio" Stocks

This component of the passive investor's portfolio is the largest, and for a good reason. It's the one that should perform the best over time, with the caveat that other investment ideas may perform far better over short periods of time.

Investments in this category should ideally include a basket of 10 to 15 stocks that have had a history of continually increasing their dividends over the last 20 years. This weeds out most stocks that are highly susceptible to economic cycles and instead focuses on companies with strong brands or consumer goods. The number of stocks (10–15) means that even if you're wrong about an individual stock, the other names should more than allow the portfolio to hold up over time.

Such stocks may include companies like Proctor & Gamble (PG), Johnson & Johnson (JNJ), Campbell Soup (CPB), J. M. Smucker (SJM), Intel (INTC), Microsoft (MSFT), and the like.

Dividend-growth stocks may, over the short term, fluctuate a bit. Over longer periods, increasing dividends should keep stock prices going up as well. You also have the opportunity to reinvest a growing cash dividend if your focus is on long-term growth as opposed to an immediate cash payout.

·   10 Percent: Commodities

On the other end of the spectrum from dividend-growth stocks are highly cyclical investments in commodities. This should include physical gold and silver as a potential insurance against unexpected and extreme market events. Having

5 percent of your wealth in the physical metals should provide more than enough insurance. Most investors hold either no gold or too much, and 5 percent in physical gold strikes a solid balance against unlikely but devastating financial events unfolding.

Beyond that, funds and individual stocks can offer a way to invest in base metals, precious metals, and agriculture while offering better liquidity and lower volatility than commodity options and futures.

Just remember, the commodity market is highly cyclical. Right now it's generally out of favor after starting off the new millennium with a powerful rally. So it's important that passive investors stick with commodity investments that have little leverage, just to stay safe and debt-free.

If you feel strongly about the prospects of a small exploratory commodity company, such as an early stage gold mining concern, you would include such a high-risk venture in this category. Again, most investors have either no commodity exposure or too much so just make sure you strike a balance and have a little without going overboard.

· 10 Percent: High-Yielding Investments

The forecast for the passive investor calls for interest rates to gradually rise. That's bad news for bond investors, but some high-yielding areas could fare well as fears of rising interest rates cause prices to lower enough to keep yields high.

Rather than try to earn money from savings or bonds, it will be necessary to invest in a few high-yielding investments to provide for a moderate level of income in the average investment portfolio.

With the expectation that interest rates will remain low, a 15 percent stake in some high-yielding investments such as leveraged funds, foreign bond funds, or mortgage REITs should provide current income for those who need it. If you want to stay fully invested, high-yielding plays will allow you to rapidly generate cash for new investments.

· 10 Percent: Energy and Infrastructure

The coming years may see the need for increased government stimulus and efforts to create more jobs for those thrown out of work. Some of this will include spending on infrastructure, which, in the United States, is rapidly aging. This also includes energy infrastructure, such as new oil pipelines and wells.

Globally, the need for new energy and infrastructure is surging in emerging market economies, offering global companies the chance to increase their revenue in coming years.

Ideally, you should invest in this area with income from pipeline master limited partnerships (MLP) investments and large established firms. But this category should include growth opportunities as well, particularly in small-cap "wild-catter" energy companies, akin to the junior gold miners in the commodity section.

· 10 Percent: Real Estate

For some investors, an allocation toward real estate should include an actual rental property outside a primary residence.

As outlined in the chapter in real estate, the real returns of a property purchased with 20 percent cash down can produce effective returns of more than 15–20 percent in markets that were hit the hardest during the financial crisis and are still struggling to get back to new highs.

Being long leveraged in real estate (i.e., having a mortgage) is also an effective way to diversify *away* from the dollar. If there is a serious pickup in inflation, fixed mortgage payments will decline in real terms over time, while rents can be raised. Of course, if inflation picks up, so will taxes, fees, and repair costs over time.

One major caveat with this investment: a second property will require some work on the part of the owner. For those with the skill and acumen to make small repairs and the like, however, it can still be a good deal. The worse the property, however, the more likely expensive repairs will be a regular feature.

Given the backlog of foreclosures, it shouldn't be too difficult to find a property in great condition trading at a price that throws off great cash flow each month in bombed-out property markets.

If you're looking for truly lazy and passive returns, you would be wise to invest in real estate investment trusts (REITs), which has cash yields of more than 5 percent. Some major REITs have rallied so much since the bottom of the financial crisis that they can no longer even clear this dividend-yield threshold.

Relative to individual property ownership, REITs offer diversification across several properties, and take care of management so you don't have to. The only thing a lazy investor needs to is sit back and collect cash payments every 90 days.

5 Percent: Cash and Cash Equivalents

Cash offers a cushion against the unknown. Outside of precious metals, it serves as an insurance policy against a catastrophic market correction that sends other asset classes falling. It also offers you the "dry powder" necessary to take advantage of extreme opportunities that may take place from time to time over the coming years.

In the area of cash, the US dollar tends to rally when other assets are selling off. As I write, the dollar is strengthening, but

US stocks are also hovering near all-time highs. However, the long-term trend of the dollar is to decline in value. Thus cash positions are important, but bear in mind that you'll be raising cash often by closing out profitable trades first and usually with a new investment in mind. Cash, during the investment years, should be put to use as much as possible. You'll only want to increase your cash holdings the closer you get to retirement.

Since we're building a portfolio loaded with dividend-growth companies, and some high-yielding investments and real estate holdings that throw off income, starting with a 5 percent allocation in cash may sound low, but it will grow over time as the income continues to roll in.

· 15 Percent: High-Growth Companies and Speculative Opportunities

Here's where you get to have some fun. This part of the portfolio is where you can gamble, speculate, or do just about anything else. That's why the allocation is so small. Any investor can stomach a loss of 10 percent of their portfolio. If you want to truly "play" the markets, this section is where most of your focus should lie.

Want to buy call options on a hot biotech company? It goes here. Do you want to invest in some sector seeing rapid growth? It goes here. Forex trades? Yep, here. A friend or family member has a business idea and needs some starting capital? It goes here too. Passive investors who are more interested in sleeping well at night can instead use this part of the portfolio to "hedge" against the other positions.

These hedging activities include selling covered calls against open positions, using long-dated options to profit from a potential market decline, or using inverse funds to profit from an overvalued area of the market that is likely to correct soon.

Speculative opportunities may also include options to go "short" the market. Whether this is done by selling short shares of an individual security or by using put options against a stock or index, a small short position can hedge the overall portfolio from an unexpected pullback.

This is where you can make some mistakes. It won't affect the overall portfolio too much. Any big successes can, however, have a tremendous effect on your overall wealth.

This is also the category that can include high-flying growth names, such as Apple (AAPL), Alphabet (GOOG), or NVIDIA (NVDA). Because this portfolio is designed to navigate choppy investment waters over the next few years only, growth stocks may experience exceptional turbulence. That's why their allocation in this model portfolio is more limited.

Hopefully, by now, the overall advantage of this hypothetical portfolio should be clear: it should perform best when left alone. Dividend growth in the biggest component of the portfolio should provide increasing income over time, and other, smaller portfolio positions may provide better short-term returns in a given year.

Dividend-growth stocks should be relatively insulated from short-term economic gyrations. Commodity investments should capture the next bull move and hedge against potential inflation. Real estate and high-yielding investments will throw off cash like gangbusters. You get the idea.

You have the opportunity to invest in assets that are both loved and hated right now. Over time, the assets that are loved will become hated—and vice versa. But the passive investor will own a little bit of everything to capture the best possibility of outperforming the market with the risk spread around *and while having to make as few trades as possible.*

If you don't want to be *completely* lazy, you should also use these hypothetical allocations as a guideline. Over time, the fluctuation of asset values will cause these areas to change significantly in value.

You may want to sell areas that appreciate the most to reinvest in areas that have underperformed. The passive investor portfolio, as is, is simply designed to start at this allocation level and see how the markets play out. By rebalancing this portfolio annually, you'll be able to take profits on areas that did well and put more capital into investments that are down with the expectation that they'll turn around in time.

There are some disadvantages that I'd be remiss if I didn't mention. This portfolio may not protect against extreme events. Individual components may have unforeseeable business risk. A bout of sudden inflation or deflation may adversely affect the portfolio, which is designed in part to assume low to moderate inflation and only gradually rising interest rates for the next few years.

And of course, there's nothing wrong with preaching caution for caution's sake.

If you're interested in building such a portfolio, you should take into account short-term market moves when you invest. A good idea is to break down a few investment ideas in each category. You can then add positions regularly—say, every month over the course of a few months—rather than invest all at once.

For most investors looking to follow this portfolio, only a few changes will be needed. Others may have to start from scratch. Either way, it can be done easily and quickly.

Appendix A

A Quick Guide to Personal Finance

WHEN IT COMES TO INVESTING, managing your personal finances goes a long way to powering your overall returns. While everyone has a unique situation thanks to tax rates, property taxes, income, and tax brackets and deductions, there are a few general principles at work that are nearly universally applicable.

To be able to invest, for instance, you need capital. That means money free between your income and your expenses. Mathematically, it looks like this:

$$\text{Income} - \text{expenses} = \text{free capital to invest.}$$

It's that simple. Spend less than you earn, and you'll be on the road to generating enough capital to start investing. It also means you'll have cash on hand to deal with any of life's uncertainties that crop up.

Here's where it gets tricky: How quickly do you want to start? I started investing in individual stocks with just $2,000. But you could start with even less if you're using a program like a dividend reinvestment plan (DRIP), which many publicly traded companies offer for a low fee.

That can get you on the road to individual investing with some Core Portfolio–style stocks. If you're just starting off and have a job, however, I recommend by starting with tax-advantaged retirement accounts.

Retirement Accounts: Making the Most of Your 401(k) and IRAs

Hopefully you're taking advantage of your company's 401(k) program. Even if you can't contribute much, at least try to make some contributions regularly, because those plans offer a few opportunities.

First, there's a tax advantage. Money in a 401(k) program is pretax income. So your total tax bill is lower if you invest in a 401(k) program. That's a particularly good deal as you get into higher tax brackets.

Next, many companies offer at least some kind of matching. If you're not taking advantage of a company 401(k) match, you're leaving part of your total compensation on the table. Yet surveys have shown that only about 43 percent of employees take advantage of such plans to begin with.

Finally, investing in a 401(k) plan means you're more likely to stay the course during a market correction. The Investment Company Institute, which tracks 401(k) trends, found that "in 2008 only 3.7 percent of participants stopped contributing to their accounts. In addition, most participants maintained their asset allocations, with 14.4 percent changing the asset allocation of their account balances and 12.4 percent changing their contribution investment mix."

Because 401(k) contributions come out of paychecks regularly, you can invest in a broad range of categories without trying to time the market or pick specific stocks. Automating the investment process is a great first step, especially when going from working for a living to generating assets that can provide for your financial needs in the future.

With dozens of choices in the average corporate 401(k) plan, you should start with a stock market index fund, ideally one that follows the S&P 500 Index due to its size and number of positions. You'll also want to find the index fund with the lowest expense ratio. Index funds are passive funds by nature, so instead of paying a few percent annually—which can reduce your total returns by more than six figures over the course of an investment lifetime—your fees should be only 0.1 or 0.2 percent. A few index funds have even lower annual expense ratios, but those are comparatively rare.

Not every 401(k) plan is perfect, and no doubt at some point you'll want a vehicle where you can make individual stock trades. That's where individual retirement accounts (IRAs) and Roth IRAs come into play.

The difference between the two types of IRAs is whether the initial contributions are pretax (IRAs) or post-tax (Roth). If you don't pay taxes going in (regular IRA), then you'll have to pay taxes going out in retirement. If you pay taxes going in (Roth), you don't have to pay taxes on distributions in retirement.

If you expect to be in a low tax bracket in retirement, an IRA is the way to go. If you expect to be in a higher tax bracket or otherwise have substantial income, a Roth is the better bet here. As with many aspects of personal finance, there's no right answer that I can give—it depends on your expectations for retirement.

In either case, with an IRA, as long as the money stays in the account before you reach retirement age (starting at age 59 and a half), the dividends and capital gains will accrue tax-free. That's a tremendous advantage during your working years!

Finally—and this is the best part about an IRA or Roth IRA as compared to a 401(k) plan—while you won't get employer matching, you'll be free to invest in individual stocks. You don't have to invest in a fund if you don't want to. Given the fact that IRA contributions are limited to such small sums, however, investors buying individual stocks here should focus on Core Portfolio stocks with a dividend-growth flavor.

Keeping Expenses Low

As with investing, I'm almost always looking for a deal. That helps keep expenses down. If I can keep my expenses down, then I have more capital to invest. It's as simple as that. It doesn't matter what I'm buying; I want the best deal possible. When I can get a good deal, it means stocking up. When something I need is on sale at the grocery store, I know that it'll be on sale again in a few months. So I can buy a lot now, and just as I'm running out, I'll have the opportunity to buy more. What's the point of waiting to buy quality stocks if I'm going to pay full price for steak the next time I'm at the grocery store?

Being frugal isn't the same thing as being cheap. Your preretirement years are also where you live the most of your life. Make the most of it. Enjoy things from time to time—just don't go overboard. There are a few things worth paying up for, particularly items like shoes and mattresses, where you're spending a large amount of your time using. But you can still be comfortable without being lavish.

Housing is one area where expenses can vary wildly. I live in a 28-year-old house that was pretty typical of middle-class America at the time it was built: it's a three-bedroom, two-bath home with a modest yard and about 1,600 square feet of living space. I don't need more room, nor do I envy those who have more. While I could afford a bigger place (in reality, bigger mortgage payments), my needs are met.

Yes, a home can be a good investment if you buy right. But you won't see any income unless you rent out a room. You won't realize any gains until you sell. From a cash-flow perspective, home ownership isn't just an expense; it's likely the biggest one you'll have. There's no need to chase home prices (or square footage) up.

Debt: Only as Good as How You Use it

Some personal finance gurus argue that debt is bad. Some argue that it's good. My view is that the truth lies in the middle. That's because debt isn't good or bad per se. It's another financial tool. Like a hammer or a firearm, whether it's good or bad depends on how it gets used.

In the area of debt, I would avoid high-interest-rate debt such as credit card debt. While I make most payments on credit cards, I pay in full each month. And I've found reward cards that offer me the best benefits—that's just another way of making debt work in my favor. Another advantage of using credit cards is that the provider usually has your back. If you have a problem with a merchant, your credit card company may be able to provide a solution, whereas you'd be out of luck had you paid with cash or debit.

A home mortgage, particularly at today's interest rates, is good debt. It's secured by property, and if you get a fixed rate, you can get a large debt financed at 30 years. It's a great deal today, although that means in turn you're likely paying more for housing if you move. If you can, put down at least 20 percent so you don't have to pay additional home mortgage insurance—that's a policy where you're paying but another party, the bank, benefits if you lose your home.

I'm mixed on car debt. While I'm generally against it, rates are pretty reasonable right now. And a car is a tool that gets you to and from a job. If you don't need it, great. If you do need it, get the lowest rate possible and buy used. Cars lose over half their value within 2–3 years on average. Buying used, even if it's a few years old, will save a tremendous amount of money compared to leasing.

Debt for investing? I wouldn't bother. That's because there are plenty of double-leveraged ETFs you could buy instead, so someone else has to deal with the leverage. Or if you think a particular industry will do well, you should look toward buying a company with the highest amount of debt. That's using their leverage to benefit you. It also means the most you can lose on a trade is 100 percent of your money, and not a theoretically infinite amount.

The bottom line is that debt is generally another expense. It's best to keep your expenses down, but there are some debts worth having, like a mortgage or possibly a car loan.

Appendix B

*Core Investment Themes: 15 Principles
to Keep in Mind When Investing*

AS AN INVESTOR, I FIND that I'm often thinking not just in terms of the trade but in terms of how governments and laws can impact such a trade. While that hasn't been the primary focus of my investment career, the outside influences of governments and third parties on the stock market cannot be denied. Here are a few themes I keep in mind as secondary considerations when investing so that I'm looking beyond just the trade in front of me.

1. Government's nature is to expand; this expansion will lead to chaos (and opportunities).
   - It is the nature of all individuals and groups to acquire as many resources as possible at the lowest cost in terms of energy.
   - Central banks have been created to allow governments to spend beyond their means and promise things they otherwise couldn't. This breeds inflation.
   - Government is always "behind the curve" when it comes to new technologies, so before the chaos of bad legislation, there will be the opportunity of other investments.

TAKEAWAY FOR INVESTORS:

Invest in various countries to "diversify" from your own government's actions. Invest across asset classes to avoid the pain of taxes and other regulatory burdens. The technology sector is promising because a product or service has to exist and be popular enough before the government can come in and start taxing or regulating it too.

2. "Crisis" always creates calls for more government action, but most actions are taken to merely keep to the status quo (or as close as possible) and to "kick the can down the road."

   · Crisis means opportunity too. At this point of what Sir John Templeton called the "point of maximum pessimism,"[1] you can reap the largest rewards.

TAKEAWAY FOR INVESTORS:

Successful investing is largely a function of getting into the right asset at the right time—namely, while it's the most unloved. Identifying potential crises and likely policy responses by government are also good for long-term investing. Many of the case studies in this book have started from the premise of looking at the current market conditions at a given time and finding some of the most unloved and out-of-favor opportunities.

3. You must pay attention to long-term and short-term effects. Wall Street and politicians focus on the short term, leading to poor long-term decisions.

   · Most investors focus on the short term, following the idea of John Maynard Keynes that "in the long run, we're all dead."[2] These investors focus on short-term capital gains, which leads to larger risk and larger volatility.

   · Frederic Bastiat's 1850 essay "That Which Is Seen, and That Which Is Not Seen" is a great elucidation of this phenomenon. In short, there are secondary effects to any tax, regulation, or other government move that will only play out over time. While the government can create problems in the short term that lead to good investment ideas, you should also invest with the long term in mind.

· The long-term effects of short-term decisions and actions are "unintended consequences."

TAKEAWAY FOR INVESTORS:

You can look at the short-term effects of a government policy or Wall Street darling stock and see a problem developing. This prevents you from joining investment bubbles and also allows you to step in after the chaos ensues to pick up assets for pennies on the dollar.

4. Gold is the optimal store of value in chaotic and turbulent times.

· Gold is the closest thing to a stable currency that mankind has discovered. It can't be artificially created (counterfeited), and no one has figured out how to transmute any more abundant element into gold (manufacture it).

· Its value will fluctuate with the supply coming onto the market and demand from the market, just as any currency's value will fluctuate based on supply and demand. In the short term, central banks can also add to their holdings or sell and impact returns here outside the free market.

· While gold prices could be manipulated by central banks, physical bullion is still the antifiat currency play.

· As a baseline, 5 percent of one's wealth should be in hard gold bullion, irrespective of where everything else goes. When gold is in a bull market, another 5 percent of your wealth in gold stocks can provide market-smashing returns.

- Silver has a lot of the same characteristics with less government influence but is also susceptible to industrial demand.

  TAKEAWAY FOR INVESTORS:

  In the age of economic chaos, gold reigns supreme. Like any asset, it won't go up or down in a straight line. It's also important to note that as the concerns that send investors flocking to gold fade, it will decline.

5. Fiat currencies are subject to political pressure for an "easy way out."

   - A fiat currency is a sophisticated method of theft used by politicians and central bankers to steal from their citizens via inflationary policies.
   - Not all fiat currencies move the same way at the same time. Wealth can be preserved—possibly enhanced—if there is a constant rotation from overvalued to undervalued fiat currencies.
   - You can profit through international currency differentials, but you must always remember that all currencies are money-by-fiat with no true underlying value.

   TAKEAWAY FOR INVESTORS:

   You must rely on more than just cash to preserve and grow your wealth. This includes international investments in stocks, bonds, precious metals, and Forex trading when extreme opportunities present themselves. International investing can also provide a safe outlet to get diversified out of a currency but also provide growth and income potential.

6. The US government's current policy is destructive: destroy the dollar in the hope of growing the economy.

   - Any "rescue," whether of banks, consumers, or certain industries, is merely an acceleration of the long, slow destruction of the dollar. The trillions of dollars in stimulus since 2008 have arguably failed to grow the economy (especially relative to the growth after other crises), and today's unemployment numbers only look good because millions have given up on finding full-time jobs. Interest rates are near zero, only gradually rising,[3] and policymakers are at a loss for better solutions.

TAKEAWAY FOR INVESTORS:

You can predict the inflationary and easy-money policies of central bankers. Now more than ever, American investors must diversify into countries capable of competently growing their economies without resorting to extreme measures to do so.

7. This time is *not* different—be a student of history.

- When someone says, "This time it's different," run the other way.
- History is rife with examples of those who profited immensely from following countertrends and doing the opposite of the herd.
- This is a core investment principle for any market at any time. Always have a set exit strategy in place and stick to it.

TAKEAWAY FOR INVESTORS:

The markets have seen it all already. You should always have a strategy in place to get out of investments that take a turn for the worse.

8. Three sigma events happen more frequently than Wall Street wants you to know (e.g., the 1987 market crash, the tech bubble crash, the housing crash).

- Recognize that, no matter how well an investment is thought out and analyzed, there is always the possibility of an exogenous event that can cause an investment to tank.

- Investment or asset protection methods that don't take a potential "worst case scenario" into account—no matter how unlikely it seems—can ultimately fall apart.
- Investments often divert substantially in value from reality. If you stay grounded in reality, you should do well in the long run.

TAKEAWAY FOR INVESTORS:

Stay away from "the next big thing." Whether it's tech stocks with no profit potential for five years or real estate being priced at record-breaking levels, the "next big thing" tends to become the next big crash. (The only exception is if *you* know it's the next big thing and *nobody else* does.)

9. Markets are irrational.
- "Mr. Market" is a pendulum, always swinging from fear to greed, and is therefore never fully rational. If the market does appear rationally priced, that's because it is either moving from extreme fear to extreme greed or vice versa.
- The market is made up of individuals. Most individuals aren't rational either. Run, don't walk, from an investment advisor who tells you an investment is a "sure thing."

TAKEAWAY FOR INVESTORS:

Sometimes, it's best to just sit tight and wait for the market to display the next extreme. That's why you want to have core trades in your portfolio that can give you solid returns and a decent income while you wait for those opportunities.

10. Wall Street is a rigged game. Brokers are fundamentally salesmen, not analysts. And they usually have "inventory" their bosses tell them to sell.
- The efficient market hypothesis (EMH) is the intellectual theory for the actions of most traders and the bulk

of the money on Wall Street. It is inherently flawed and riddled with false presumptions, all in the name of creating a "rational" market.

- All of us have conflicts of interest, and every person makes his choices based on rigging the transaction in his own favor.
- The wise person looks ahead with an eye toward the long term and realizes that it's in one's own self-interest to make every exchange a win-win exchange by telling the truth, keeping your word, and delivering on promises.
- Crooked money managers are also part of the "rigged" game. Diversify your money managers. Most individuals, armed with the right advice, can use a low-cost brokerage and manage most of their wealth themselves.

TAKEAWAY FOR INVESTORS:
Stay skeptical with your investments—and the people running them.

11. Everyone has an agenda.
- Caveat emptor: trust but verify.
- Consider the source of an idea and follow the money. The largest lobbying group in the world is the National Association of Realtors. No wonder lending standards during the housing boom were ignored by congressional overseers!
- This includes members of Congress as well. One of the biggest cheerleaders for the leverage at Fannie Mae was Barney Frank. He was also one of the biggest recipients of campaign funds from the now-bankrupt firm.
- Many in the media who offer financial advice tell you to follow the herd.

Takeaway for investors:
It's better to lead the herd than follow the herd. It's even better to avoid getting trampled by doing the opposite of the herd.

12. Despite the harm caused by governments, they'll give you tax benefits for investing if you know where to look. Take full advantage of them.

- You can utilize 401(k) plans and various IRA programs to invest in nearly every major asset class with substantial tax benefits.
- Investments grow faster when their compounding isn't interrupted every year by the tax man.
- You can invest in various assets like real estate investment trusts (REITs) and master limited partnerships (MLPs) to substantially boost your dividend income in a low-yield world.
- Current long-term capital gains tax rates and dividend tax rates make it better to be an investor than an employee.

Takeaway for investors:
Take full advantage of any plan the government offers you (but pursuant to other concepts listed above, be sure to diversify into other areas as well).

13. A poorly regulated market is better than one rampant with corruption.

- The SEC was repeatedly warned about the Ponzi scheme run by Bernard Madoff. They ignored those warnings. Other regulatory agencies have also ignored similar warnings in their area of expertise.
- "Regulatory capture" creates perverse incentives for regulators to be lax in exchange for jobs in the industry

they were supposed to be regulating. Changes must be made.

· The government's core role is to provide law and order. That means it must enforce contracts, weed out con artists, and do so in a way that impedes as little as possible on the freedom of individuals to decide what's best for them.

TAKEAWAY FOR INVESTORS:

You should vote with your money in a diversified group of countries and exchanges that follow the rule of law and create a level playing field.

14. Remember Sturgeon's law: 90 percent of everything is crud.

· Most of what the market generates is short-term noise. Learn to filter it out. Remember, all investors at some time or another will fall prey to their emotions. A hefty dose of skepticism provides an optimal lens for making decisions.

· Don't accept what others say at face value; trust but verify.

· People hold crud because they expect someone else to come along with a higher price to bid it away. Bubbles start when the quality goes downhill and the quantity ramps up.

TAKEAWAY FOR INVESTORS:

Identify holes in the analyses of others, determine where bubbles may be forming, and find pockets of unloved values. Find safer, alternative ways to profit. Avoid leverage on assets loved by the crowd. Don't be afraid to get out of a position that's done well if it looks like it's becoming a crummy investment.

15. There's no such thing as a free lunch.

· Government can't simply create wealth or jobs through taxation or debt-financed government spending or tariffs. Any such thing comes at the expense of whatever would have been created by the private sector if left alone and unmolested.

· Markets that are outperforming cannot do so indefinitely.

TAKEAWAY FOR INVESTORS:

Keep a close eye on the markets. Be aware of where there may be an opportunity to buy and when it may be time to take profits or even go short.

In conclusion, be willing to pay up for quality investments. High-quality companies command high premiums for their franchises compared to lower-quality companies. But in an age of chaos, sell-offs may allow you to pick up phenomenal qualities at a decent price.

Appendix C

A Sample Investment Checklist

BEFORE YOU GO AND MAKE a trade, stop for a moment and think about how a potential investment fits into the following criteria:

☐ Is this a *core trade*, a *commodity trade*, a *short trade*, or something more complex?

☐ What does the company do? Can you explain it to a kindergartner?

☐ What is the company's moat? How strong is it?

☐ What are the risks? Consider the market, industry, company, competition, and valuation.

☐ What are the historical and projected growth rates of the company?

☐ Have the business's earnings been consistent throughout a relevant time period?

☐ Does the company meet your financial metric criteria for its industry?

☐ Does the company meet your balance sheet criteria for its industry?

☐ Does the company have sufficient cash flow to continue operations without outside funding?

☐ Is management focused on long-term success or short-term success?

☐ Does management have some meaningful stake in the company?

☐ What is the estimated per-share value for this company?

☐ What price is a sufficient discount to the per-share estimate of its value to provide a sufficient margin of safety?

☐ Does this investment fit in with your overall portfolio goals? If there is some overlapping, what will you sell?

☐ What criteria will you use to determine that the investment is no longer buying?

Epilogue

INVESTING IS A JOURNEY, NOT a destination. The path that that journey takes will largely stem from you. This journey isn't to a fixed place, marked on a map. It's ever-changing, reflecting the dynamic of the market process and the inevitable economic chaos of today's complex economy. And you'll need to keep moving to continue—which means you'll need to find new trades, new investments, and recognize when to leave an old investment behind.

Like everyone else, I'm still learning. We all are. There will be more success and more failure along the way. And we'll see new situations and opportunities develop in the future that we could have never foreseen. Fortunately, there are some ideas and principles that, when applied, can throw the returns of the average investor far ahead of the curve. In short, they're the things that prepare you for when those unpredictable opportunities present themselves.

Those principles still work in a variety of situations, as has been seen with various trades I've made for myself and my newsletter subscribers over the past 20 years across the investment universe.

Whatever your financial goals, having the flexibility to find out-of-favor trades, including those that involve going short the market or individual stocks at times, will get you there. It may take patience. Not every trade will win. But if you look at a trade with how bad the possible downside is in mind, you'll be better prepared to profit.

Stay safe and stay out of debt, and getting rich will take care of itself.

Notes

Chapter 1
1 https://www.forbes.com/sites/rajsabhlok/2013/08/13/death-of-the
-pc-time-to-kiss-your-computer-goodbye/#c4d725948395.

Chapter 2
1 http://www.grubstreet.com/2016/02/folgers-coffee-popularity.html.

Chapter 3
1 https://en.wikipedia.org/wiki/List_of_banks_acquired_or
_bankrupted_during_the_Great_Recession.
2 Ibid.

Chapter 4
1 http://www.nytimes.com/2003/01/24/business/mcdonald-s-posts
-its-first-loss-and-lowers-outlook-for-growth.html.
2 http://money.cnn.com/2001/10/19/companies/planet/.
3 http://247wallst.com/investing/2010/09/09/the-13-worst-recessions
-depressions-and-panics-in-american-history/3/.

Chapter 5
1 http://www.berkshirehathaway.com/letters/1997.html.

Chapter 7

1 http://alphahistory.com/weimarrepublic/1923-hyperinflation/.

Chapter 8

1 https://www.chk.com/documents/media/publications/annual
   -report-2003.pdf.
2 http://www.reuters.com/article/us-chesapeake-mcclendon-profile
   -idUSBRE8560IB20120607.
3 http://www.nasdaq.com/article/chesapeake-ceo-aubrey-mcclendon
   -resigns-what-now-cm212458.

Chapter 9

1 http://www.politifact.com/truth-o-meter/statements/2008/jan/25/
   rudy-giuliani/us-is-saudi-arabia-of-coal/.
2 http://www.ngsa.org/download/issues/
   NGCleanestBurningFossilFuel.pdf.
3 http://fortune.com/2016/07/20/why-donald-trump-wont-bring
   -coal-jobs-back-to-west-virginia/.
4 http://nypost.com/2016/03/14/hillarys-vow-to-kill-coal-miners-jobs
   -finishes-a-vast-democratic-betrayal/.

Chapter 10

1 http://www.popularmechanics.com/technology/infrastructure/
   a14375/this-quarter-mile-cargo-ship-is-the-largest-ever/.

Chapter 13

1 http://money.cnn.com/2014/11/27/news/opec-oil-prices/index.html.

Chapter 14

1 https://en.wikipedia.org/wiki/VIX.

Chapter 15

1 http://money.cnn.com/2013/02/15/investing/herbalife-stock-icahn/
   index.html.
2 https://en.wikipedia.org/wiki/In_re_Amway_Corp.

3 https://www.ftc.gov/news-events/press-releases/2016/07/herbalife
-will-restructure-its-multi-level-marketing-operations.

Chapter 16
1 http://www.businessinsider.com/google-earnings-2012-10.
2 Ibid.

Chapter 17
1 http://us.spindices.com/index-family/real-estate/sp-corelogic-case
-shiller.
2 https://fred.stlouisfed.org/series/MORTGAGE30US.

Appendix B
1 http://www.investopedia.com/university/greatest/johntempleton.asp.
2 https://en.wikiquote.org/wiki/John_Maynard_Keynes.
3 http://www.shadowstats.com/.

Index

About the Author

Andrew Packer is a senior financial writer with Newsmax Media. He is currently author of the *Insider Hotline* and *Financial Braintrust* services, as well as author of the monthly newsletter *Resolute Wealth Letter*. His prior books include *Aftershock's High Income Guide: Discover the Powerful Secrets to Achieving Superior Returns*; *Uncharted: Your Guide to Investing in the Age of Uncertainty*; and *Insider's Dossier: How to Use Legal Insider Trading to Make Big Stock Profits*. He has previously worked in private equity and real estate research and has a background in economics. His weekly blog can be found on Fridays at www.moneynews.com.

The Franklin Prosperity Report

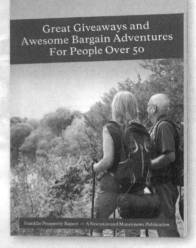

How an Ordinary Man Turned $8,000 Into $7 Million

GET HIS SECRETS TO WEALTH TODAY

The Dividend Machine, written by Bill Spetrino, has been hailed by Mark Hulbert of the *Hulbert Financial Digest* as the #1 low-risk newsletter in the industry, based on performance.

Bill Spetrino

One look at the portfolio tells you why the newsletter deserves such acclaim. It is filled with companies from all across the globe that hold a dominant position in their industries. And these companies use that dominant position to generate piles and piles of cash, which they return in shareholders in the form of dividends.

But not just any dividend payer will qualify for inclusion in **The Dividend Machine** portfolio. In order to be added to the portfolio, it must meet a very stringent set of criteria that Bill has set forth. And it must have one final factor above all: it must be priced right.

The Dividend Machine is a culmination of more than 20 years of Bill's personal experience investing in high-quality dividend stocks. In fact, it is the exact same investing philosophy that allowed Bill to walk away from his 9-to-5 job at the age of 42 and live comfortably on the income from his investments alone.

As a member of **The Dividend Machine**, you will be partners with Bill. For only $97.95 per year, you will be able to study his analysis, learn from his insight, and gain knowledge from his vast investment experience. In short, you will have one of the world's leading experts in dividend investing working with you side-by-side every month. And each month Bill will recommend a new opportunity to consider adding to your personal Dividend Machine portfolio.

Partner with Bill, Go To:
Newsmax.com/TDMDebt